FOREWORD BY DR. KATRINA FERGUSON

ENTER God's REST

Lessons From Mary And Martha

JAMES W. FERGUSON

ENTER GOD'S REST - Lessons from Mary and Martha
by James W. Ferguson

www.JamesWFerguson.com

ISBN: 9780998169026-20-00
Printed in the United States of America

FIG Publishing * 1500 Beville Road, #606 * Daytona Beach, FL 32114

www.FIGPublishing.com * info@FIGPublishing.com

WWW

TABLE OF CONTENTS

Bless the Lord, O my soul: and all that is within me, bless his holy name. Bless the Lord, O my soul, and forget not all his benefits. (Psalms 102:1-2)

All Scripture is quoted in King James Version unless otherwise noted.

GOD'S INTIMATE LOVE

And such trust have we through Christ to God-ward.
(II Corinthians 3:4)

From the rising of the sun
To the going down of the same
You, Father God
Are to be praised

You are magnified throughout the land
You are glorified throughout the land
You are honored throughout the land

You are the Almighty God

You are the Only true God

You are the Great King (Malachi 1:14)

It is
You that we praise
You that we honor
You that we worship

All glory to You

You are the God of love

You love us so much that when we were enemies (Rom. 5:10)
You gave your only begotten son
To bridge the otherwise unbridgeable gap (II Cor. 5:18)
Between sinful man and holy God

You are the God of the overflow

You prepare a table before us in the presence of our enemies
You anoint our heads with oil
You make our cups overflow (Psalm 23)

Your expressed desire
Is to open up the windows of heaven
And to pour out a blessing
That there is not room for us to receive it

You have made us God's vineyard
You have made us God's building (I Cor. 3:9)
You have made us God's temple (II Cor. 6:16)

You are the unchangeable God (Mal.3:6)
You are the faithful God
You are the promise keeper
You have given us all things through Jesus (I Cor. 3:21-22)
Because of You we reign in this life through Jesus (Rom. 5:17)
Because of You we have eternal life through Jesus

Glory to You Almighty God!

You are the God of peace (Rom. 15:33)
Your love has given us peace with God
Now and forever
For there is no fear in love
For perfect love casteth out fear (I John 4:18)

You are the God of Hope (Rom. 15:13)
Nothing can separate us from Your love (Rom. 8:39)
Your love has given us a place
Of intimacy with you

Father God

Thank You
For the intimacy of your love
You knew us before
We were formed in our mother's wombs
You know us by name (John 10:3)
You know our needs before we ask
You answer our prayers before we even call (Isaiah 65:24)

Thank you, Father God
For the intimacy of your love

You know us and you love us
Not just the dressed for church us
Not just the dressed for work us
Not just the trying to be attractive us
Not just the best foot forward us

You know us and you love us
You know the us that we fight so hard to suppress us
You know the us that we express when we are angry us
You know the us that we try to hide us

Your goodness, Father God
Is such that You know each part of us
And You love all of us

Glory to God

Thank you, Heavenly Father
For the intimacy of your love

Our left hand may not know what our right hand is doing
When we give alms
But the intimacy of the Love of God
Sees what we do in secret
And rewards us openly

When we enter into our prayer closet
Shut the door
And pray to the Father in secret
The intimacy of the Love of God
Sees in secret
And rewards us openly

The intimacy of the love of God
Is such that God's knows what we need before we ask

When we fast in secret
The intimacy of the love of God
Sees and rewards us openly

The intimacy of the love of God
Makes us new creations in Christ Jesus

The intimacy of the love of God
Changes us
From the inside out
The intimacy of the love of God
Transform us
From the inside out
Into the image of Jesus

Glory to God!

The intimacy of the love of God
Allows us to have the mind of Christ

The intimacy of the love of God
Allows our physical needs to be met
Allows our emotional needs to be met
Allows our mental needs to be met
Allows our spiritual needs to be met
Even when we don't know what our needs are

The intimacy of the love of God knows

All glory to You
Almighty God

The intimacy of the Love of God
Reassures us
That we are accepted in the beloved

There are no last-minute revelations
That can change who we are in Christ
There is nothing that has remained hidden
That can be uncovered in some final security check
There is no unpaid bill
That we have to hope doesn't show up on the credit check

The intimacy of the Love of God
There is no condemnation (Rom. 8:1)

Everything was already known when God declared his love
Everything that happened in the past and would happen in the future
Was already known when God declared his love
Everything was already known when God made us accepted in the beloved

Nothing that we have done can change who we are in Christ
Nothing that we have done can change whose we are in Christ
As Christ is
So are we

Thank you, Father
For the intimacy of the Love of God
God sees all
God knows all

Thank you, Father God
That neither death, nor life, nor angles, nor principalities,
Nor powers, nor things present, nor things to come
Nor height, nor depth, nor any other creature,
Shall be able to separate us from the love of God,
Which is in Christ Jesus our Lord.
(Romans 8:38-39)

Father God
We worship You
We magnify You
We thank You

In the name of Jesus
We pray to you

Amen

James W. Ferguson

FOREWORD

James Ferguson is not just a highly educated attorney, he is a brilliant communicator who spends much of his time researching, writing, and reading. As a result, each time he speaks, he succinctly cuts to the core of the matter, bringing clarity and understanding to every interaction. He exemplifies the definition of genius with class, allure, and above all, validity. Today, as I compose the foreword to this incredible book, I am genuinely excited to introduce you to *"Enter God's Rest: Lessons from Mary and Martha."*

My excitement over this work is not only because of my great admiration of Mr. Ferguson, but because this book contains divine revelations which I believe can literally change the world and bring people together, from all backgrounds and cultures, around a deeper revelation of what it means to *Enter God's Rest.* His devotions are incredible, and like his speaking, draw our attention back to the core of the matter, faith, and belief in God for all things, including our daily itineraries. This book will help you further develop your relationship with Jesus Christ, a critical process in the life of any Christian.

This is the story of two sisters, Mary and Martha, and speaks to the busyness, the unrest, the lack of peace and consequently the lack of rest, to which we have all been victim. It uncovers the lessons hidden in the story of the busy sister verses the sister who chose to sit at the feet of Jesus. It is a rare instance that a book has left such an impact on my life. It took me a couple sittings to complete it, not because it was hard to read, but because I had to deal with the reality of me seeing more of Martha in me than Mary. (ouch) Reading this book has assisted me in clarifying my priorities and resetting my agenda, realizing that investing in myself by partaking of God's love and peace lies more in having faith in God than in the work of my hands. (Double ouch)

In conclusion, I know his research and insights will enlighten you in many ways, as it has me. With busy lifestyles, routines, and family obligations, many are skeptical as to whether God still speaks and if so, what He is saying. At a time when the popular opinion seems to outweigh both the written and spoken Word of God, you will find that the clarity you seek comes from entering into His rest … not busying yourself with the noise of your life. Expect great moves of God as you read and apply what you learn here. In other words, read it and reap!"

~Dr. Katrina Ferguson, Entrepreneur,
Inspirational Speaker, Life Coach
www.KatrinaFerguson.com

*"I am a problem solver for **W**hat **H**urts **Y**ou, and a catalyst for your why. I coach leaders and entrepreneurs on how to increase their influence and value in the Kingdom, while achieving financial freedom, without compromising the things they value most."*

CHAPTER I

PRIORITIES

Now it came to pass, as they went, that he entered into a certain village: and a certain woman named Martha received him into her house. And she had a sister called Mary, which also sat at Jesus' feet, and heard his word. But Martha was cumbered about much serving . . . (Luke 10:38-40)

The difference in the behaviors of Martha and Mary is significant. Mary sitting and hearing. Martha working. Mary "heard his word" but Martha was "cumbered about much serving." Mary heard Jesus because she was focused on Jesus. Martha didn't hear Jesus because she was focused on other things. In verse 38, Martha received Jesus into *her* house, but by verse 40, she didn't hear him. How can a woman who knows who Jesus is, receive Jesus into her home, work to make sure that Jesus and everyone else with him is fed and taken care of and yet not *hear* Jesus when he spoke?

The same way we do.

When the Bible speaks of "hearing" Jesus, it is not only referring to physically hearing his voice. We know that neither the physically deaf nor the physically dead can physically hear, but the Bible says they "heard" Jesus.

> *[39] Jesus said, Take ye away the stone. Martha, the sister of him that was dead, saith unto him, Lord, by this time he stinketh: for he*

> *hath been dead four days. [40] Jesus saith unto her, Said I not unto thee, that, if thou wouldest believe, thou shouldest see the glory to God? . . . [43] And when he thus had spoken, he cried with a loud voice, Lazarus, come forth. [44] And he that was dead came forth bound hand and foot with graveclothes: . . . (John 11:39-44)*

Even when the Bible does speak of physical "hearing" it is not only referring to hearing sound. It is speaking of accepting and believing the Word of God, which always leads to receiving from God.

> *Why do ye not understand my speech? even because ye cannot hear my word. (John 8:43)*

Accepting and believing is what allowed many physically deaf people to "hear" Jesus and receive the healing of physical hearing. It is what allowed physically dead people to "hear" Jesus and return to life. And it is what allowed spiritually dead people to be born again. Hearing and believing is what allowed the miraculous to take place in the lives of believers then, and it is what allows the miraculous to take place in the lives of believers now.

> *Jesus answered and said to them, "Go and tell John the things you have seen and heard: that the blind see, the lame walk, the lepers are cleansed, the deaf hear, the dead are raised, the poor have the gospel preached to them. (Luke 7:22, NKJV)*

After telling a parable or teaching a principle Jesus would often say "He that hath ears to hear, let him hear."

After telling the parable of the sower Jesus said:

> *"He who has ears to hear, let him hear."*
> *(Matthew 13:9, NKJV)*

After telling the parable of the wheat and the tares, Jesus said:

> *"He who has ears to hear, let him hear."*
> *(Matthew 13:43; Mark 4:9, NKJV)*

When John the Baptist was in prison, he sent two of his disciples to ask Jesus:

> *"Are you the one who was to come, or should we expect someone else?"*
> *(Matthew 11:3, NIV)*
>
> *[7] As John's disciples were leaving, Jesus began to speak to the crowd about John: {saying} [14] And if ye will receive it, this is Elias, which was for to come. [15] He that hath ears to hear, let him hear.*
> *(Matthew 11:7-15)*

The Bible makes clear that the crowd heard Jesus with their physical ears. They were in his presence and they asked him questions. Just as Martha was in his presence and asked him questions. So, Jesus wasn't speaking of physical hearing when He said, "He who has ears to hear, let him hear." He was speaking of hearing with spiritual ears. The

Bible says, *"God is a Spirit."*[1] And Jesus told his disciples *"The words that I speak to you, they are spirit, and they are life."*[2] We have to hear God in our spirit, with our "spiritual" ears. Spiritual hearing requires a move away from judging what God says,[3] to accepting and believing what God says.

> *So shall my word be that goeth forth out of my mouth: it shall not return unto me void, but it shall accomplish that which I please, and it shall prosper in the thing whereto I sent it. (Isaiah 55:11)*

> *Why do ye not understand my speech? Even because ye cannot hear my word. (John 8:43)*

Married couples often complain that their spouse doesn't "hear" them. Many people cry out for help before they get into trouble. But cries for help are easily missed when the parent, the child, the spouse, the friend or whoever is listening can't hear the loneliness, the fear, the pain, or the warnings in the speaker's voice. In short, they may hear the speaker's words, but they don't "hear" the speaker.

Too many people today attempt to carry on a conversation while sending a text, reading an email, or doing something else at the same time. Some, call it multi-tasking.

---

[1] *John 4:24*

[2] *John 6:63*

[3] *For the wisdom of this world is foolishness to God. (I Corinthians 3:19, NLT)*

Others, call it rude. But by whatever name, it makes it difficult to "hear" the speaker. Good parents give loving, necessary, and sound advice to teenage children every day. But often the immature mind of the child that thinks they are an adult can't "hear" the parents.[4]

Why didn't Martha hear Jesus?

The answer may help to explain why so many of us, men, women and children of God, brothers and sisters of Christ, fail to hear God even when we are in His presence. The answer may help to explain how two people can have the same parents; or come up in the same house; or belong to the same church; or sit in the same pew; or read the same Bible; or go to the same Bible study; or get saved on the same day; and one person hears God and their earthly life is changed forever. And the other person loves God, but their earthly life is simply one struggle after another, or lurches from one crisis to another. God loves them both but one of them just can't hear him.

There is a level of hearing God that determines what happens to us when we leave this world:

> *[24] Verily, verily, I say unto you, He that heareth my word, and believeth on him that sent me, hath everlasting life, and shall not come into condemnation; but is passed from death unto life. [25] Verily, verily, I say unto*

---

[4] This is often caused, in no small part, by parents treating minor children as if they were their friends instead of their children. And later the parent wonders why the child does not know his or her place. But that too is another sermon.

you, The hour is coming, and now is, when the dead shall hear the voice of the Son of God: and they that hear shall live. (John 5:24-25)

And there is a level of hearing that determines what happens to us while we are in this world:

[24] Then He said to them, "Take heed what you hear, With the same measure you use, it will be measured to you; and to you who hear, more will be given. [25] For whoever has, to him more will be given; but whoever does not have, even what he has will be taken away from him." (Mark 4:24-25, NKJV)

The more we hear God and use what we hear, the more God will tell us, and the more our lives will prosper.

For as you know him better, he will give you, through his great power, everything you need for living a truly good life; he even shares his own glory and his own goodness with us. (2 Peter 1:3, TLB)

But if we don't hear God, we won't simply stand still in life, we will go backwards. This is illustrated in the parable of the talents. The servant that used the money well was given more. As for the servant that used the money poorly, even what he had was taken away and given to the servant that used the money well.

For the man who uses well what he is given shall be given more, and he shall have abundance. But from the man who is unfaithful, even what little responsibility he

> *has shall be taken from him.*
> *(Matthew 25:29, TLB)*

God wants us to prosper. God did not send His son to suffer and die for us to be miserable until we get to heaven. Jesus said:

> *I came that they may have and enjoy life, and have it in abundance (to the full, till it overflows). (John 10:10, AMP)*[5]

Lurching from one struggle after another, or from one crisis to another is not enjoying life. Living in debt, unable to pay your bills, is neither enjoying life nor living in abundance. The Bible says God *". . . hath pleasure in the prosperity of his servant,"*[6] and that *"it is God who works in you both to will and to do for His good pleasure."*[7] If God has pleasure in the prosperity of his servants, you can rest assured that he has pleasure in the prosperity of his children!

Behold what manner of love the Father has bestowed on us, that we should be called children of God! (1 John 3:1, NKJV)

---

[5] *See also Luke 18:29-30: [29] And he said unto them, Verily I say unto you, There is no man that hath left house, or parents, or brethren, or wife, or children, for the kingdom of God's sake, [30] Who shall not receive manifold more in this present time, and in the world to come life everlasting.*

[6] *Psalm 35:27 (NKJV)*

[7] *Philippians 2:13 (NKJV)*

CHAPTER II

GOD'S LOVE IS NOT FOR SALE

And who could ever offer to the Lord enough to induce him to act? (Romans 11:35, TLB)[8]

Whenever we read or hear words, we form a mental image or utilize a mental frame of reference to understand what we've read or heard. So, when the Bible speaks of God the Father, we all form our own conscious or subconscious mental images. And we use our images to interpret this description of God and the nature of our relationship with God. This can be a foundational choke point in our relationship with God. This is a problem even for the "well churched" because of the proclivity to conflate our relationship with God, and our relationship with Jesus. For while we are indeed joint heirs with Christ, we are always children of God.

Selah!

One of the unfortunate consequences of so many children growing up without fathers - whether the male lives in the home or not - is that it skews their view, our view, of God the Father. Most of us think of fathers in terms of what

---

[8]*See also Romans 11:35 (AMP) Or who has first given God anything that he might be paid back or that he could claim a recompense?*

we've seen, heard, or experienced of natural fathers. The general belief is that fathers - like most authority figures – are displeased when we misbehave. And behaving is generally defined as something we physically "do" such as obeying the rules. Whether out of fear or respect, the key is generally to act in a certain manner. We act the right way, and we get the reward. Whether the reward is a money, approval, a new car, love, or simply not getting yelled at, really doesn't matter. The process is the same. First, we act/do and then get a reward. Or, even more often, we do something "wrong" then we have to do something "right" before we can get the withheld reward. And that experience, generally shapes how we see God and how we see our relationship with God. Consequently, we have little expectation of receiving from God because we often feel that we are not deserving based on our manner of behaving. But this entire belief system of behavior then reward is earthly, not heavenly, and results in a skewed view of God.

> *For this world's wisdom is foolishness {absurdity and stupidity} with God, for it is written, He lays hold of the wise in their {own} craftiness. (I Corinthians 3:19, AMP)*

The belief system of act then reward may be an accurate reflection of how things work with many earthly fathers, but it is exactly the opposite of how things work with our heavenly Father.

God always gives first!

When we were separated from God, before we were born again, God gave his Son to die for us with no preconditions:

> *But God commendeth his love toward us, in that, while we were yet sinners, Christ died for us. (Romans 5:8)*

> *[16] For God so loved the world, that he gave his only begotten Son, that whosoever believeth in him should not perish, but have everlasting life. [17] For God sent not his Son into the world to condemn the world; but that the world through him might be saved. (John 3:16-17)*

At the pool of Bethesda, God gave first:

> *[5] Now a certain man was there who had an infirmity thirty-eight years. . .. [8] Jesus said to him, "Rise, take up your bed and walk." [9] And immediately the man was made well, took up his bed, and walked. . ..*
> *[14] Afterward Jesus found him in the temple, and said to him, "See, you have been made well. Sin no more, lest a worse thing come upon you." (John 5:5-14, NKJV)*

When the woman was caught in adultery, God gave first:

> *[3] The teachers of the law and the Pharisees brought in a woman caught in adultery. They made her stand before the group [4] and said to Jesus, "Teacher, this woman was caught in*

> *the act of adultery. [5] In the Law Moses commanded us to stone such women. Now what do you say?" . . . [7] . . . {Jesus} said to them "If any one of you is without sin, let him be the first to throw a stone at her." . . . (John 8:3-7, NIV)*

> *[9] At this, those who heard began to go away one at a time, the older ones first, until only Jesus was left, with the woman still standing there. [10] Jesus straightened up and asked her, "Woman, where are they? has no one condemned you?" [11] No one, sir," she said. "Then neither do I condemn you," Jesus declared. "Go now and leave your life of sin." (John 8:9-11, NIV)*

From before the beginning of time until now, God always gives first!!

> *Long ago, even before he made the world, God chose us to be his very own through what Christ would do for us; he decided then to make us holy in his eyes, without a single fault – we who stand before him covered with his love. (Ephesians 1:4, TLB)*

Nowhere in the Bible does Jesus tell anyone to go earn what they came to receive. Jesus only does what God does.[9] So whoever has seen Jesus has seen God.[10] God always gives first.

But God demonstrates his own love for us in this: While we were still sinners, Christ died for us. (Romans 5:8, NIV)

[9] *See John 5:19*

[10] *See John 14:9*

CHAPTER III

DON'T FRUSTRATE THE GRACE OF GOD

{C}hrist's righteousness makes men right with God... (Romans 5:18, TLB)

For he hath made him to be sin for us, who knew no sin; that we might be made the righteousness of God in him. (II Corinthians 5:21)

When we have the wrong image of God, we waste time toiling to earn our righteousness instead of enjoying time reveling in our righteousness.[11] Often, we mistakenly try to earn righteousness with God, and favor from God, by using the Ten Commandments. Which "*are good when used as God intended. But they were not made for us, whom God has saved.*"[12] When we work to earn our righteousness with God, we frustrate the grace of God and the crucifixion of Christ.

> *Christ is become of no effect unto you, whosoever of you are justified by the law; ye are fallen from grace. (Galatians 5:4)*

---

[11] *The thief comes only in order to steal and kill and destroy. I came that they may have and enjoy life, and have it in abundance (to the full, till it overflows) (John 10:10, AMP)*

[12] *I Timothy 1:8-9 (TLB)*

> *For God took the sinless Christ and poured into him our sins. Then, in exchange, he poured God's goodness into us!*
> *(II Corinthians 5:21, TLB)*

The Ten Commandments represent the old covenant which didn't work to save anybody then and doesn't work to save anybody now.

> *[7] The old agreement didn't even work. If it had, there would have been no need for another to replace it. [8] But God himself found fault with the old one . . .*
> *(Hebrews 8:7-8, TLB)*

God put the old covenant aside and replaced it with a new covenant containing better promises.

> *God speaks of these new promises, of this new agreement, as taking the place of the old one; for the old one is out of date now and has been put aside forever. (Hebrews 8:13, TLB)*

> *. . . the new agreement that he passes on to us from God contains far more wonderful promises. (Hebrews 8:6, TLB)*

When we persist in striving to show ourselves righteous before God based on rules, we are enslaving ourselves, and trying to earn our righteousness with God.

> *But now that you know God – or rather are known by God – how is it that you are turning back to those weak and miserable principles?*

Do you wish to be enslaved by them all over again? (Galatians 4:9, NIV)

You are trying to find favor with God by what you do or don't do on certain days or months or seasons or years. (Galatians 4:10, TLB)

I fear for you, that somehow I have wasted my efforts on you. (Galatians 4:11, NIV)

And to the extent we realize we haven't kept the rules – laws, commandments, etc. – just like with the earthly norms, we don't expect to receive the promises of God.

For the more we know of God's laws, the clearer it becomes that we aren't obeying them; his laws serve only to make us see that we are sinners . . . (Romans 3:20, TLB)

Hence, we have little faith or expectation of receiving from God. But this all rests on the wrong image of God. And it denies the power of the crucifixion of Christ. Neither God's love, nor God's favor, nor God's gift of righteousness, is based on our efforts. It is based on God's grace.

Being justified freely by his grace through the redemption that is in Christ Jesus. (Romans 3:24)

God is love. And God loves us so much that he gave his son to die for us before we were saved, before we were righteous or "good enough,"[13] before we acknowledged him as Lord, and before we acknowledged his way of doing things as right. Nothing can separate us from the love of God.[14] God didn't give the law so that we could keep it and earn his love or earn salvation. God gave the law so that we could see that we were sinners.

> *For the Law never made anything perfect . . . (Hebrews 7:19, AMP)*
>
> *Well then, why were the laws given? They were added after the promise was given, to show men how guilty they are of breaking God's laws. But this system of law was to last only until the coming of Christ, . . . (Galatians 3:19, TLB)*
>
> *Now do you see it? No one can ever be made right in God's sight by doing what the law commands. For the more we know of God's laws, the clearer it becomes that we aren't obeying them; his laws serve only to make us see that we are sinners (Romans 3:20, TLB)*

---

[13] *[4] But when the time came for the kindness and love of God our Savior to appear, [5] then he saved us – not because we were good enough to be saved but because of his kindness and pity - . . . (Titus 3:4-5, TLB)*

[14] *[38] For I am convinced that neither death nor life, neither angels nor demons, neither the present nor the future, nor any powers, [39] neither height nor depth, nor anything else in all creation, will be able to separate us from the love of God that is in Christ Jesus our Lord (Romans 8:38-39, NIV).*

> *Therefore no one will be declared righteous in his sight by observing the law; rather, through the law we become conscious of sin.*
> *(Romans 3:20, NIV)*

Albert Einstein reportedly said that God doesn't play dice.[15] In other words whatever God has said or created was not by chance or by accident. Every word and act of God is on purpose and serves a purpose.

> *And we know that all things work together for good to them that love God, to them who are called according to his purpose.*
> *(Romans 8:28)*

> *[2] And his disciples asked him, saying, Master, who did sin, this man, or his parents, that he was born blind? [3] Jesus answered, Neither hath this man sinned, nor his parents: but that the works of God should be made manifest in him. . . (John 9:2-3)*

> *[6] When he had thus spoken, he spat on the ground, and made clay of the spittle, and he anointed the eyes of the blind man with the clay, [7] And said unto him, Go, wash in the pool of Si-lo-am (which is by interpretation, Sent.) He went his way therefore, and washed, and came seeing. (John 9:6-7)*

---

[15] *Einstein: A Hundred Years of Relativity*, Andrew Robinson

God's purpose cannot be overthrown.

> *The Lord of hosts has sworn, saying "Surely, as I have thought, so it shall come to pass, And as I have purposed, so it shall stand: (Isaiah 14:24, NKJV)*

For too long we've misunderstood the purpose of the law and have tried to misuse it to become righteous. The law cannot make us righteous because that was not God's purpose for the law. God's purpose for the law was to make us conscious of our sins. But that is not the end of the story because God has made righteousness available to us apart from the law.

> *[21] But now a righteousness from God, apart from law, has been made known, to which the Law and the Prophets testify. [22] This righteousness from God comes through faith in Jesus Christ to all who believe. There is no difference, [23] for all have sinned and fall short of the glory of God, [24] and are justified freely by his grace through the redemption that came by Christ Jesus. (Romans 3:21-24, NIV)*

> *{F}or it was through reading the Scripture that I came to realize that I could never find God's favor by trying – and failing – to obey the laws. I came to realize that acceptance with God comes by believing in Christ. (Galatians 2:19, TLB)*

> *Where is boasting then? It is excluded. By what law? Of works? Nay: but by the law of faith. (Romans 3:27)*

> *For what saith the scripture? Abraham believed God and it was counted unto him for righteousness. (Romans 4:3)*

Righteousness does not come by trying to follow the 10 Commandments. Righteousness does not come by works. Righteousness comes by having faith/believing in the Son of God Jesus Christ.

> *But to him that worketh not, but believeth on him that justifieth the ungodly, his faith is counted for righteousness (Romans 4:5)*

> *For in the gospel a righteousness from God is revealed, a righteousness that is by faith from first to last, just as it is written: "The righteous will live by faith." (Romans 1:17, NIV)*

Righteousness is a gift. We cannot earn it through work. We cannot earn it through cooking dinner. We cannot earn it through preaching. We cannot earn it through any of the busyness that we say we are doing for God. It is in the midst of our well-intended busyness that we are most likely to miss the voice of God.

Why didn't Martha hear Jesus?

The *Amplified Bible* described Martha as overly occupied, too busy and distracted.[16] Just like Martha became caught up in her well-intended busyness, we can become so caught up in our well-intended busyness that we forget that the very purpose of God is to heal the sick:

> *. . . The Pharisees asked Jesus, "Is it legal to work by healing on the Sabbath day?"*
> *(Matthew 12:10, TLB)*

We can become so caught up in our well-intended busyness that we forget that the very purpose of God is to save the lost:

> *And when the Pharisees saw it they said to His disciples, "Why does your Teacher eat with tax collectors and sinners?"*
> *(Matthew 9:11, NKJV)*

We can become so caught up in our well-intended busyness that we attack others who don't ignore the presence of God. Mary was sitting at the feet of the Lord, and listening to Him, when Martha said to Jesus:

> *". . . doesn't it seem unfair to you that my sister just sits here while I do all the work? Tell her to come and help me."*
> *(Luke 10:40, TLB)*

---

[16] *Luke 10:40 (AMP)*

We can become so caught up in our well-intended busyness that we may even attack others who worship God in a manner that is pleasing to God.

> *[7] A woman came to Him having an alabaster flask of very costly fragrant oil, and she poured it on His head as He sat at the table. [8] But when His disciples saw it, they were indignant, saying, "Why this waste? [9] For this fragrant oil might have been sold for much and given to the poor." (Matthew 26:7-9, NKJV)*

> *But Jesus, fully aware of this, said to them, Why do you bother the woman? She has done a noble (praise-worthy and beautiful) thing to Me. (Matthew 26:10, AMP)*

We can become so caught up in our well-intended, self-directed, busyness that we end up with what the Bible calls misdirected zeal.

> *[2] I know what enthusiasm they have for the honor of God, but it is misdirected zeal. [3] For they don't understand that Christ has died to make them right with God. Instead they are trying to make themselves good enough to gain God's favor . . . (Romans 10:2-3, TLB)*

We can become so caught up in our well-intended busyness that we completely miss or ignore the word, the voice, the purpose, and/or even the presence of God.

> *[5] Now a certain man was there who had an infirmity thirty-eight years. . . . [8] Jesus said to him, "Rise, take up your bed and walk." And immediately the man was made well, took up his bed, and walked. And that day was the Sabbath. [10] The Jews therefore said to him who was cured, "It is the Sabbath; it is not lawful for you to carry your bed." [11] He answered them, "He who made me well said to me, 'take up your bed and walk.'"*
> *[12] Then they asked him, "Who is the Man who said to you, "Take up your bed and walk'?" (John 5:8-12, NKJV)*

They didn't start by celebrating that the man had been healed after 38 years!! They didn't even start by asking him who healed him after 38 years!! They were more concerned about a violation of the rules than they were about a movement of God. Similar things happened when Jesus healed the woman who hadn't been able to stand up straight for 18 years, and when Jesus healed the man who had been blind from birth.

> *{T}he leader of the synagogue, indignant because Jesus had healed on the Sabbath, said to the crowd, There are six days on which work ought to be done; so come on those days and be cured, and not on the Sabbath day. (Luke 13:14, AMP)*

> *Therefore some of the Pharisees said, "This Man is not from God, because He does not keep the Sabbath." (John 9:16, NKJV)*

We can become so caught up in our well-intended, self-directed, busyness that we think our so-called working for God, is more important than listening to God. Such self-righteousness not only pushes us away from God, it makes us judgmental and pushes us away from God's people.

> *". . . doesn't it seem unfair to you that my sister just sits here while I do all the work? Tell her to come and help me."*
> *(Luke 10:40, TLB)*
>
> *[41] But the Lord said to her, "Martha, dear friend, you are so upset over all these details! [42] There is really only one thing worth being concerned about, Mary has discovered it - and I won't take it away from her!*
> *(Luke 10:41-42, TLB)*

In fact, we can get things so twisted around in our well-intended busyness that we question whether the Lord who died for us even cares about us.

> *. . . Lord, don't you care that my sister has left me to do the work by myself?*
> *(Luke 10:40, NIV)*[17]

---

[17] Questioning whether God really cares for us is the open door for doubt, unbelief and sin. It is the same subterfuge Satan used to beguile Eve in the Garden of Eden.

It becomes easier to avoid misdirected zeal when we remember that our righteousness is a gift from God. We cannot earn it. We cannot add to it.

I do not frustrate the grace of God: for if righteousness come by the law, then Christ is dead in vain. (Galatians 2:21)

CHAPTER IV

DELIGHT YOURSELF IN THE LORD

There is really only one thing worth being concerned about, Mary has discovered it - and I won't take it away from her! (Luke 10:42, TLB)

Mary's sole concern was listening to and receiving from Jesus. And that, according to Jesus, was the one thing worth being concerned about. That makes perfect sense because every good and perfect gift comes from God.

> *[16] Don't be deceived, my dear brothers. [17] Every good and perfect gift is from above, coming down from the Father of the heavenly lights, who does not change like shifting shadows. (James 1:16-17, NIV)*

Life, peace, provision, and power, all result from listening to and receiving from Jesus.

> *[20] My son, give attention to my words; Incline your ear to my sayings. [21] Do not let them depart from your eyes; Keep them in the midst of your heart; [22] For they are life to those who find them, And health to all their flesh. (Proverbs 4:20-22, NKJV)*

> *You will keep him in perfect peace whose mind is stayed on thee: because he trusteth in thee. (Isaiah 26:3)*
>
> *Delight yourself in the Lord and he will give you the desires of your heart. (Psalms 37:4, NIV)*
>
> *{T}o those whom God has called . . . Christ the power of God and the wisdom of God. (I Corinthians 1:24, NIV)*

God doesn't love us any less when we don't listen. But when we don't listen, we walk in less of everything that God has for us. The choice is ours. Jesus loved Martha,[18] and didn't love her any less because she wasn't listening to him. He didn't even tell her she was wrong for what she was doing. He recognized her efforts and her concerns. But He did say that Mary made a better choice. Just like Martha and Mary we too have a choice. We can choose to continue our well-intended, self-directed, busyness. Or we can choose to listen to Jesus. Martha chose to be busy. Mary chose to listen. Jesus said Mary made the better choice.

> *[41]"Martha, Martha," the Lord answered, "you are worried and upset about many things, [42] but only one thing is needed. Mary has chosen what is better . . . (Luke 10:41-42, NIV)*

---

[18] *Now Jesus loved Martha, and her sister, and Lazarus. (John 11:5)*

Martha was well intended. Just as a lot of our self-directed work is well intended, practical, and appears to make sense. But when we choose to listen to Jesus, we may find that a lot of what makes sense to us may not be God's best for us.

Martha was worried about preparing food. In the *Book of Matthew,* Jesus said:

> *[31] Therefore take no thought, saying, What shall we eat? Or, What shall we drink? Or, Wherewithal shall we be clothed? [32] (For after all these things do the Gentiles seek:) for your heavenly Father knoweth that ye have need of all these things. [33] But seek ye first the kingdom of God, and his righteousness; and all these things shall be added unto you. (Matthew 6:31-33)*

The disciples were worried about forgetting food.

> *[8] Which when Jesus perceived, he said unto them, O ye of little faith, why reason ye among yourselves, because ye have brought no bread? [9] Do ye not yet understand, neither remember the five loaves of the five thousand, and how many baskets ye took up?*
> *[10] Neither the seven loaves of the four thousand, and how many baskets ye took up? (Matthew 16:8-10)*

Peter was worried about the wind.

> *[28] And Peter answered Him and said, "Lord, if it is You, command me to come to*

> *You on the water." [29] So He said, "Come." And when Peter had come down out of the boat, he walked on the water to go to Jesus. [31] But when he saw that the wind was boisterous, he was afraid; and beginning to sink he cried out, saying, "Lord, save me!" (Matthew 14:28-31, NKJV)*

Peter understood the power of the presence of God. Once he knew it was God, ("Lord, if it be you . . .") he had the courage to get out of the boat in the midst of the turbulent sea,[19] and he had the faith to walk on the water. The wind was contrary before he got out of the boat. And the wind was contrary while he was walking on the water. There is absolutely no correlation between the condition of the wind and man's ability to walk on water. Peter began to sink because he shifted his focus away from Jesus and unto the storm.

The Bible says:

> *He that observeth the wind shall not sow; . . . (Ecclesiastes 11:4)*

Just as a storm has no role in man's ability to walk on water, success for Christians is not dependent on any external physical condition. It is dependent on our internal spiritual condition. If the spiritual force of faith is present, then Christians can do all things through faith in Christ.

---

[19] *But the boat was by this time out on the sea, many furlongs {a furlong is one-eighth of a mile} distant from the land, beaten and tossed by the waves, for the wind was against them. (Matthew 14:24 AMP)*

> *I can do all things through Christ which strengthenething me. (Philippians 4:13)*

Faith is a spiritual force with a physical effect. Faith changes how we see and interact with the natural world, and changes how we see and interact with God. The spiritual force of faith can change physical things and change our physical capabilities in the natural world.[20] Through faith in Jesus, there is healing. By faith the woman with the issue of blood knew that if she could just touch the hem of His garment, she would be made whole. After she was made whole, Jesus confirmed that it was her faith that had made her whole.[21]

Through faith in Jesus, there is peace. The Bible says Martha was cumbered about;[22] upset over details;[23] worried and upset about many things;[24] and feeling that she was being treated unfairly.[25] But there are no such descriptions about Mary being disturbed. Mary was not disturbed because

---

[20] *See Hebrews Chapter 11*

[21] *See Luke 8:43-48*

[22] *Luke 10:40*

[23] *Luke 10:41 (NLT)*

[24] *Luke 10:41 (NIV)*

[25] *Luke 10:40 (NLT)*

Mary was focused on Jesus. And in Jesus – Jehovah-shalom[26] - there is peace.[27]

> *You will keep him in perfect peace, whose mind is stayed on You, because he trusts in You. (Isaiah 26:3, NKJV)*

Through faith in Jesus, there is hope.

> *And his name shall be the hope of all the world. (Matthew 12:21, TLB)*

Through faith in Jesus, there is power.

> *And {so that you can know and understand} what is the immeasurable and unlimited and surpassing greatness of His power in and for us who believe . . . (Ephesians 1:19, AMP)*

> *In conclusion, be strong in the Lord [be empowered through your union with Him]; draw your strength from Him [that strength which His boundless might provides]. (Ephesians 6:10, AMP)*

Through faith in Jesus, there is wisdom.

---

[26] *See Judges 6:24*

[27] Shalom is the Hebrew word mostly understood to mean peace. But shalom, according to *Strong's Concordance*, also means completeness, wholeness, health, peace, welfare, safety soundness, tranquility, prosperity, perfectness, fullness, rest, harmony, the absence of agitation or discord.

[24] But to those who are called, whether Jew or Greek {gentile}, Christ [is] the Power of God and the Wisdom of God.
(I Corinthians 1:24, AMP)

But our busyness can choke out our power, provision, peace, wisdom and all that is available to us in the name of Jesus.

Now he who received seed among the thorns is he who hears the word, and the cares of this world . . . choke the word.
(Matthew 13:22, NKJV)

Jesus is the Word of God made flesh.

In the beginning was the Word, and the Word was with God, and the Word was God.
(John 1:1, NKJV)

For there are three that bear witness in heaven: the Father, the Word, and the Holy Spirit; and these three are one.
(I John 5:7, NKJV)

When we stop focusing on Jesus, when we stop focusing on the word, we lose our peace, we lose our hope, we lose our wisdom, and we lose our power. When we shift our focus away from Jesus, we shift away from the very things that we need.

. . . our power and ability and sufficiency are from God. (II Corinthians 3:5, AMP)

> *[3] In him lie hidden all the mighty, untapped treasures of wisdom and knowledge. (Colossians 2:3, TLB)*

When we focus on Jesus, our busyness may suffer but our business won't.

> *[5] But Simon answered and said to Him, "Master, we have toiled all night and caught nothing; nevertheless at Your word I will let down the net." [6] And when they had done this, they caught a great number of fish, and their net was breaking. [7] So they signaled to their partners in the other boat to come and help them. And they came and filled both boats. (Luke 5:5-7, NKJV)*

Whenever we focus on anything besides Jesus, we are on a path of unsustainable self-support, self-righteousness and self-defeating unbelief. When we believe that our business, busyness or self-righteousness is the rewarder we are no longer walking in faith. Those who come to God must believe that "he is and that he is a rewarder of those that diligently seek Him."[28] All self-righteousness is works.

> *[2] . . . Did you receive the Spirit by the works of the law, or by the hearing of faith? [3] Are you so foolish? Having begun in the Spirit, are you now being made perfect by the flesh? (Galatians 3:2-3, NKJV)*

---

[28] *Hebrews 11:6*

> *[8] For by grace you have been saved through faith, and that not of yourselves; it is the gift of God, [9] not of works, lest anyone should boast. (Ephesians 2:8-9, NKJV)*
>
> *{N}ot by works of righteousness which we have done, but according to His mercy He saved us, . . . (Titus 3:5, NKJV)*

When we walk in self-righteousness we become like the younger son and his older brother in the parable of the prodigal son. The younger son thought, after wasting his money in riotous living, that because of his behavior he no longer deserved to be a son.[29] This is self-righteousness. The older son thought, because of his good behavior, he deserved the benefits of being a son. This is also self-righteousness. Neither son understood that their son-ship was never something that they earned or deserved. They were born into son-ship.

Similarly, as Christians we can never earn or deserve our positions as children of God. We are born-again into our positions as children of God. And we retain our positions as children of God through the grace of God. When the younger son asked to be a servant the father gave him all the marks of son-ship (ring, robe, and sandals), killed the fatted calf, and celebrated the return of his son. Just like the father gave the son all the marks of sonship, God has granted us all the marks and privileges of son-ship.

---

[29] *See Luke 15:17-21*

> *Behold, what manner of love the Father hath bestowed upon us, that we should be called the sons of God: . . . (I John 3:1)*

The perspectives of both sons are analogous to the perspectives of many well-meaning, God loving, Christians. Like the younger son, too many Christians are striving to be servants of God instead of living as children of God.

> *{H}e is not served by human hands, as if he needed anything, because he himself gives all men life and breath and everything else. (Acts 17:25, NIV)*

While the younger son was living in lack, the older son was living in abundance. But instead of enjoying the fruits of being a son, the older brother labored and harbored the resentment that comes from years of continually working for what he already owned.

> *'Look! All these years I've been slaving for you and never disobeyed your orders. Yet you never gave me even a young goat so I could celebrate with my friends.' (Luke 15:29, NIV)*

The older son was bitter from waiting to be given what his earthly father had already given him. Similarly, many Christians are bitter from waiting to be given what our heavenly Father has already given us. The older son was bitter from years of living, working - and worst of all - thinking, like a slave instead of feasting like a son. Too many Christians spend years living, working – and worst of all – thinking like servants instead of feasting like sons. Bitterness, frustration, resentment, and even jealousy of those who are availing themselves to God's abundance is often a result.

This is evident in the older brother and his behavior regarding the younger brother. And it is evident in Martha's behavior regarding Mary.

We often deny what is available to us, what we are entitled to receive as children of God, in order to justify our failure to walk in what God has provided. Or, in Christian parlance, we put off to the sweet by and by what the Bible says we are entitled to in the here and now.[30] Just as the father in the parable of the prodigal son said to his older son "*you are always with me, and all that I have is yours,"*[31] God is saying the same thing to his children. Everything he has is ours.

> *He who did not spare his own Son, but gave him up for us all – how will he not also, along with him, graciously give us all things? (Romans 8:32, NIV)*
>
> *Charge them that are rich in this world, that they be not highminded, nor trust in uncertain riches, but in the living God, who giveth us richly all things to enjoy. (1 Timothy 6:17)*
>
> *[28] Then Peter began to say unto him, Lo, we have left all, and have followed thee.*
> *[29] And Jesus answered and said, Verily I say unto you, There is no man that hath left house, or brethren, or sisters, or father, or mother, or wife, or children, or lands, for my*

---

[30] *See Mark 10:29-30*

[31] *Luke 15:31 (NKJV)*

> *sake, and the gospel's. [30] But he shall receive an hundredfold now in this time, houses, and brethren, and sisters, and mothers, and children, and lands, with persecutions; and in the world to come eternal life. (Mark 10:28-30)*
>
> *{T}hose who received {God's} overflowing grace {unmerited favor} and the free gift of righteousness {putting them into right standing with Himself} reign as kings in life through the one Man Jesus Christ {the Messiah, the Anointed One}. (Romans 5:17, AMP)*

The older brother in the story of the Prodigal Son was laboring as a slave when he should have been reigning as a king. The father had divided the inheritance between both sons before the younger son left with his portion. Neither son did anything to earn this inheritance. Both sons knew the inheritance had to come from their father. Similarly, as new Christians we recognize we need Christ and trust his completed work to save us. [32] We accept that we can neither deserve nor earn God's gift of righteousness. Then somehow, we begin like the older brother to think that we are entitled to our son-ship based on our good behavior. Or we begin like the younger brother to think that we are no longer entitled to our son-ship based on our bad behavior. In either case, we have fallen from grace.[33]

---

[32] *Ephesians 1:11-14*

[33] *See Galatians 5:4*

In some cases, we begin to think that as we mature in Christ we should rely less on Christ. But that is nonsensical.

> *{F}or if trying to obey the Jewish laws never gave you spiritual life in the first place, why do you think that trying to obey them now will make you stronger Christians?"*
> *(Galatians 3:3, TLB)*

If we want to grow in Christ, we must lean more on Christ:

> *[W]e grow only as we get our nourishment and strength from God.*
> *(Colossians 2:19, TLB)*

If we want to hear more from God, we must lean more on Christ:

> *[1] Long ago God spoke in many different ways to our fathers . . . [2] But now in these days he has spoken to us through his Son . . .*
> *(Hebrews 1:1-2, TLB)*

If we want to receive more from God, we must lean more on Christ:

> *But whatever is good and perfect comes to us from God . . . (James 1:17, TLB)*

If we want to walk in more of the power and boldness of God, we must lean more on Christ:

> *[29] And now, Lord, behold their threatenings: and grant unto thy servants, that*

> *with all boldness they may speak thy word, [30] by stretching forth thine hand to heal; and that signs and wonders may be done by the name of thy holy child Jesus. . . . [33] And with great power gave the apostles witness of the resurrection of the Lord Jesus: and great grace was upon them all. (Acts 4:29-33)*

The answer is always in Christ.

> *He carries out and fulfills all of God's promises, no matter how many of them there are; . . . (II Corinthians 1:20, TLB)*

He is the vine, we are the branches.[34] The Christ is the source for all things of God.

> *I ask you again, does God give you the power of the Holy Spirit and work miracles among you as a result of your trying to obey the Jewish laws? No, of course not. It is when you believe in Christ and fully trust him. (Galatians 3:5, TLB)*

The resolution to the problem is always in the Christ.

> *[5] Trust in the Lord with all your heart, and lean not on your own understanding; [6] In all your ways acknowledge Him, and he shall direct your paths. (Proverbs 3:5-6)*

---

[34] *See John 15:1-7*

> *For as you know him better, he will give you, through his great power, everything you need for living a truly good life: . . . (2 Peter 1:3, TLB)*

When we are not leaning on, trusting in, the Christ, all we have left is our own understanding. Our understanding is carnal. God is a Spirit.[35] His words are spirit.[36] Faith is a spirit.[37] And the carnal cannot understand the spiritual.

> *Because the carnal mind is enmity against God; for it is not subject to the law of God, nor indeed can be. (Romans 8:7, NKJV)*

> *The man without the Spirit does not accept the things that come from the Spirit of God, for they are foolishness to him, and he cannot understand them, because they are spiritually discerned. (I Corinthians 2:14, NIV)*

With our own understanding, we have neither ears to hear God nor eyes to see God and we limit God's ability to move on our behalf.

> *[2] . . . "Where did this Man get these things? And what wisdom is this which is given to Him, that such mighty works are performed by*

---

[35] *John 4:24*

[36] *John 6:63*

[37] *II Corinthians 4:13*

> *His hands! [3] Is this not the carpenter, the Son of Mary, and brother of James, Joses, Judas, and Simon? And are not His sisters here with us?" So they were offended at Him. (Mark 6:2-3, NKJV)*
>
> *And because of their unbelief he couldn't do any mighty miracles among them except to place his hands on a few sick people and heal them. (Mark 6:5, TLB)*

When we shift our focus from Jesus, we can get caught up in following our traditions[38] such as how we've always done things; what church we've attended; or denomination we've belonged to; how we've always prayed; and/or the opinions of those around us. Taking our eyes off Jesus is self-defeating and can happen to even the most mature Christians.

God ordained miracles, angelic visitations, and prophecies surrounded the life of John the Baptist even before he was conceived.[39] He was great in the sight of the Lord, and filled with the Holy Ghost while he was still in his mother's womb.[40] The hand of the Lord was with John from

---

[38] *"Why do Your disciples not walk according to the tradition of the elders, but eat bread with unwashed hands?" (Mark 7:5, NKJV)*

[39] *See the Gospel of Luke Chapter 1.*

[40] *Luke 1:15*

the time he was an infant.[41] It was prophesied at John's birth that he would be called the prophet of the Highest, and would go before Jesus to prepare His way.[42] John's ministry was so successful that all of Judea and Jerusalem went out to hear him preach, were baptized by him,[43] and wondered if he was the Christ. It was John who baptized Jesus. It was John who recognized that Jesus was the Savior of the world.[44] It was John who announced to the world that Jesus was the Son of God.[45] It was John who said that his job was to prepare the way so that everyone would go to Jesus.[46] It was John who, when speaking about Jesus, said: "He must increase, but I must decrease."[47] And, yet, it was John who after all of the foregoing, while languishing in prison, sent his disciples to ask if Jesus really was the Messiah.[48]

The Apostle Paul was a great man of God. He wrote significant portions of the New Testament. He started numerous churches; preached the Lord Jesus to kings and governors; raised the dead; healed the sick; cast out demons;

---

[41] *Luke 1:66*

[42] *Luke 1:76*

[43] *Mark 1:4*

[44] *Matthew 3:13-16*

[45] *John 1:29-34*

[46] *John 3:28 (TLB)*

[47] *John 3:30 (NKJV)*

[48] *Luke 7:19 (TLB)*

and when Paul's clothes were laid on the sick, they were healed and demons were cast out.[49] Paul been jailed, shipwrecked, beaten and stoned for preaching Jesus Christ is Lord.

> *[24] Of the Jews five times received I forty stripes save one. [25] Thrice was I beaten with rods, once was I stoned, thrice I suffered shipwreck, a night and a day I have been in the deep; [26] In journeying often, in perils of waters, in perils of robbers, in perils by mine own countrymen, in perils by the heathen, in perils in the city, in perils in the wilderness, in perils in the sea, in perils among false brethren;[27] In weariness and painfulness, in watchings often, in hunger and thirst, in fastings often, in cold and nakedness. (II Corinthians 11:24-27)*

In the *Book of Acts*, Paul boldly argued against the Jewish believers that said the non-Jewish believers had to be circumcised.[50] And he publicly confronted the Apostle Peter for not eating with gentiles and for acting hypocritically regarding the Jewish laws.[51] Yet, even this great man of God had Timothy circumcised in "deference to the Jews."[52]

---

[49] *Acts 19:11-12*

[50] *Acts Chapter 15*

[51] *See Galatians Chapter 2*

[52] *Acts 16:3 (TLB)*

In his later years, Paul refused to succumb to any such pressure regarding Titus.

> *[4] Even that question wouldn't have come up except for some so-called "Christians" there – false ones, really – who came to spy on us and see what freedom we enjoyed in Christ Jesus, as to whether we obeyed the Jewish laws or not. They tried to get us all tied up on their rules, like slaves in chains. [5] But we did not listen to them for a single moment, for we did not want to confuse you into thinking that salvation can be earned by being circumcised and by obeying Jewish laws. (Galatians 2:4-5, TLB)*

No matter how long we may have been saved. No matter what churches or ministries we lead or have led. No matter what church we attend or anointed leadership we sit under. No matter what spiritual or ministerial gifts we may have. No matter what miracles God may have done through us. No matter how much we may speak in tongues. No matter how much we may be filled with the Holy Ghost. No matter how important we may be in our local church. No matter how holy people tell us we are. No matter, no matter, no matter, there will be pressure to focus and move based on something other than Jesus.

> *{T}hese two forces within us are constantly fighting each other to win control over us, and our wishes are never free from their pressures. (Galatians 5:17, TLB)*

In the Bible, Barnabas encouraged the believers in Antioch "to stay close to the Lord, whatever the cost."[53] The further we are from Jesus, the more room there is for doubt and unbelief, and the further we are from all that is ours in the name of Jesus. Contrariwise, the closer we stay to Jesus (Mary sat at his feet), the more we are able to walk in all that Jesus died for us to receive.

> *Then he said to all, "Anyone who wants to follow me must put aside his own desires and conveniences and carry his cross with him every day and keep close to me!*
> *(Luke 9:23, TLB)*

There may be great theological interpretations about the meaning of "carry his cross with him every day," but "stick close to me" seems relatively simple. God who doesn't change,[54] and cannot lie,[55] told us he'd always be with us.[56] So, if we feel distant from God, it is not because God has moved. Since He will never move away from us, the only variable is whether we are consciously sticking close to Him, or letting our busyness distract us from Him. Jesus was with Martha, but she couldn't hear him because she was busy with other things. Mary heard Jesus because she was focused on

---

[53] *Acts 11:23 (TLB)*

[54] *Malachi 3:6*

[55] *Titus 1:2*

[56] *Matthew 28:20*

Jesus. As children of God, we know God's voice.[57] The closer we stick to God, the more intimate we become with his voice. And the more intimate we become with God's voice, the easier it will be for us to hear God's guidance helping us in every area of our lives.

> *But we know about these things because God has sent his Spirit to tell us, and his Spirit searches outs and show us all of God's deepest secrets. (I Corinthians 2:10, TLB)*

> *For God is at work within you, helping you want to obey him, and then helping you do what he wants. (Philippians 2:13, TLB)*

Because we have the Holy Spirit, we can listen with spiritual ears and hear with spiritual understanding.

> *Know ye not that ye are the temple of God, and that the Spirit of God dwelleth in you? (I Corinthians 3:16)*

> *{T}he spiritual man has insight into everything, and that bothers and baffles the man of the world, who can't understand him at all." (I Corinthians 2:15, TLB)*

And through the Holy Spirit, we have the mind of Christ.

---

[57] *See John Chapter 10*

> *For who among men knows the thoughts of a man except the man's spirit within him? In the same way no one knows the thoughts of God except the Spirit of God.*
> *(I Corinthians 2:11, NIV)*
>
> *For who hath known the mind of the Lord, that he may instruct him? But we have the mind of Christ." (I Corinthians 2:16)*

Delight yourself also in the Lord, and he shall give you the desires of your heart. (Psalm 37:4, NKJV)

CHAPTER V

BELIEVE GOD [58]

The work of God is this: to believe in the one he has sent. (John 6:28-29, NIV)

Jesus saith unto her, Said I not unto thee, that, if thou wouldest believe, thou shouldest see the glory of God? (John 11:40)

Belief impacts behavior.[59] For Christians, the results that come to fruition and the process leading to those results all turn on believing - or not believing - the Word of God.

> *He who believes in the Son has everlasting life; and he who does not believe the Son shall not see life; but the wrath of God abides on him. (John 3:36, NKJV)*

Jesus told his disciples to:

> *[22] . . . Have faith in God. [23] For assuredly, I say to you, whoever says to this mountain, 'Be removed and be cast into the*

---

[58] Trust in, cleave, to, and rely on what God says. *See Luke 22:67 AMP.*

[59] *See Mark 7:25-30.*

> *sea,' and does not doubt in his heart, but believes that those things he says will be done, he will have whatever he says, [24] Therefore I say to you, whatever things you ask when you pray, believe that you receive them, and you will have them. (Mark 11:22-24)*

In the absence of faith, God's ability to move on our behalf is hindered. The Bible is replete with the mighty works of Jesus. Yet, even Jesus, according to *Mark 6:1-5,* was hindered by the unbelief of the people in his hometown. Because of their unbelief, Jesus could do no mighty works there except lay his hands on a few sick folks and heal them.

Pause and think about that!

The need to believe is the same irrespective of position or station. The Bible says that the priest Zacharias and his wife Elizabeth "were both righteous before God walking in all the commandments and ordinances of the Lord blameless." [60] Zacharias asked God for a son, and God's messenger told Zacharias that God would give him a son.

> *{T}he angel said to him, "Do not be afraid Zacharias, for your prayer is heard; and your wife Elizabeth will bear you a son, and you shall call his name John. (Luke 1:13, NKJV)*

But, instead of believing God, Zacharias doubted God based on what Zacharias could do without God.

---

[60] *Luke 1:6, NKJV*

> *[18] And Zacharias said to the angel, "How shall I know this? For I am an old man, and my wife is well advanced in years." [19] And the angel answered and said to him, "I am Gabriel, who stands in the presence of God and was sent to speak to you and bring you these glad tidings. [20] But behold, you will be mute and not able to speak until the day these things take place, because you did not believe my words which will be fulfilled in their own time. (Luke 1:13-20, NKJV)*

In contrast to Zacharias, when Abraham was told that he would be given a son, Abraham believed God.

> *[18] So, when God told Abraham that he would give him a son . . . Abraham believed God even though such a promise just couldn't come to pass! [19] . . . he didn't worry about the fact that he was too old to be a father at the age of one hundred, and that Sarah his wife, at ninety, was also much too old to have a baby. [20] . . . He believed God . . . and he praised God for this blessing even before it happened. (Romans 4:18-20, TLB)*

When Mary was told that she would have a son, Mary believed God and although a virgin gave birth to a son.

> *Blessed is she who believed, for there will be a fulfillment of those things which were told her from the Lord." (Luke 1:45, NKJV)*

Everything turns on what we believe.

> *Jesus said unto him, If thou canst believe, all things are possible to him that believeth. (Mark 9:23)*

When a certain nobleman implored Jesus to go to Capernaum to heal the nobleman's son:

> *[50] Jesus said to him, "Go your way; your son lives." So the man believed the word that Jesus spoke to him, and he went his way. [51] And as he was now going down, his servants met him and told him, saying, "Your son lives!" . . . [53] So the father knew that it was at the same hour in which Jesus said to him, "Your son lives." And he himself believed, and his whole household. (John 4:50-53, NKJV)*

When the daughter of the ruler of the synagogue died, Jesus told him to believe.

> *[35] While Jesus was still speaking, some men came from the house of Jairus, the synagogue ruler. "Your daughter is dead, they said. "Why bother the teacher anymore?" [36] Ignoring what they said, Jesus told the synagogue ruler, "Don't be afraid; just believe." . . . [41] He took her by the hand and said to her, "Talitha Koum!" (which means, "Little girl, I say to you, get up!") [42] Immediately the girl stood up and walked around (she was twelve years old). (Mark 5:35-42, NIV)*

When Jesus left the little girl's house, two blind men followed him shouting and asking for mercy. Jesus didn't ask them if their behavior was perfect, he asked them if they believed.

> *[28] . . . "Do you believe I can make you see?" "Yes, Lord," they told him, "we do." [29] Then he touched their eyes and said, "Because of your faith it will happen." [30] And suddenly they could see! . . . (Matthew 9:28-30, TLB)*

Before raising Lazarus from the dead, Jesus said to Martha, "Did I not tell you that if you believed, you would see the glory to God"? [61] Then Jesus prayed, and called Martha's brother Lazarus back to life after he had already been dead for four days.[62]

What we receive is tied to what we believe.

> *And all things, whatsoever ye shall ask in prayer, believing, ye shall receive. (Matthew 21:22)*

> *Therefore I say unto you, What things soever ye desire, when ye pray, believe that ye receive them, and ye shall have them. (Mark 11:24)*

---

[61] *John 11:40 NIV*

[62] *See John 11:1-44*

> *. . . for unless you believe that I am the Messiah, the Son of God, you will die in your sins." (John 8:23, TLB)*

Blessed are those who don't doubt me. (Matthew 11:6, TLB)

CHAPTER VI

FEED ON THE WORD OF GOD

And she had a sister called Mary, which also sat at Jesus' feet, and heard his word. (Luke 10:39.)

If ye abide in me, and my words abide in you, ye shall ask what ye will, and it shall be done unto you. (John 15:7)

Shalom, often translated simply as peace, means nothing missing, nothing broken. It is the full manifestation of God's grace in our daily lives. We know there are levels of grace because the Bible encourages us to grow in grace and tells us that the apostles operated in great power when great grace was upon them.

> *But grow in grace, and in the knowledge of our Lord and Saviour Jesus Christ. To him be glory both now and forever. Amen. (2 Peter 3:18)*

> *And with great power gave the apostles witness of the resurrection of the Lord Jesus: and great grace was upon them all. (Acts 4:33)*

Shalom is a reflection of the fruits of righteousness.

> *Now he that ministereth seed to the sower both minister bread for your food, and*

multiply your seed sown, and increase the fruits of your righteousness. (II Corinthians 9:10)

The Word of God is like a seed.[63] When the Word of God is sown in us and has grown in us, fruit is always the result.[64] The Word of God and Christ are one.[65] When we are full of the word, we are full of Christ.[66] That is why Satan comes immediately to take away the word that is sown.[67] If he can't take away the word that is sown, Satan will do whatever he can do to make the word unfruitful.[68]

By continuously feeding on the word, believing the word, and moving on the word, in faith, we continuously make the word fruitful in our lives. The more we feed on the Word of God, the more we are able to hear the voice of God addressing our specific issues, needs, and desires. Too many Christians don't feed their own spirit and try to live their lives based on their understanding of what God may have said to someone else. But someone else's word may not be God's best for you. In fact, it may not be God's word for you at all. This is evidenced in the manner Jesus healed those

---

[63] *See Luke 8:11*

[64] *See Mark 4:26-32*

[65] *See John 1:1-5*

[66] *See Ephesians 4:12-13 (TLB)*

[67] *See Mark 4:14-15*

[68] *See Mark 4:14-20*

who came to him during his earthly ministry. Jesus did not heal everyone in the same way. He did not give everyone the same instructions before he healed them. Nor did he give everyone the same instructions after he healed them. Even when they had the same problems!

It was the Sabbath day and there was a man in the synagogue with a withered hand. Jesus told the man with the withered hand to stretch forth his hand, and the hand "was restored whole, like as the other."[69] It was the Sabbath day, and there was a woman in the synagogue who had a spirit of infirmity eighteen years. Jesus said to her "Woman, thou art loosed from thine infirmity." And he laid his hands on her and immediately she was healed.[70]

A man suffering from leprosy said to Jesus, "if thou wilt, thou canst make me clean." Jesus touched him and said, "I will; be though clean." And immediately the man was cleansed. Jesus told the man not to tell anyone but to go straight to the priest.[71] Ten men suffering from leprosy standing far away from Jesus cried out to him and asked for mercy. Jesus told then to go and show themselves to the priests. And as they went, they were cleansed.[72]

Jesus, beseeched by a centurion to heal his servant at home sick of the palsy, told the centurion "Go thy way; and

---

[69] *See Matthew 12:9-13*

[70] *See Luke 13:10-16*

[71] *See Matthew 8:2-4*

[72] *See Luke 17:12-14*

as thou hast believed, so be it done unto thee." And the servant was healed in the same hour. [73] The friends of a man sick of the palsy lowered him through the roof of the house where Jesus was preaching. Jesus, seeing their faith, told the man sick of the palsy that his sins were forgiven, to rise, take up his bed, and go home. And the man arose, took up his bed, and walked out.[74]

When Peter's mother-in-law was sick with a fever, Jesus touched her, and she arose and ministered unto them. [75] When a nobleman asked Jesus to come and heal his son, Jesus told him to go home, that his son was healed. The fever left the nobleman's son the moment Jesus told him his son was healed.[76]

When Jesus was in Ger-ge-senes a man possessed with two devils came to him. The devils asked Jesus, if he was going to cast them out, to let them go into a nearby herd of pigs. Jesus simply said "Go." And the devils went into the pigs, and the pigs ran violently down a steep place and into the sea.[77] Then Jesus told the man to go to his friends and tell them the great things the Lord had done for him. [78] When a

---

[73] *See Matthew 8:5-13*

[74] *See Mark 2:3-11*

[75] *See Matthew 8:14-15*

[76] *See John 4:46-53*

[77] *See Matthew 8:28-32*

[78] *See Mark 5:19*

woman of Canaan asked Jesus for mercy because her daughter was possessed by a devil, Jesus told her it wasn't right to give the children's bread to the dogs. When the woman persisted, Jesus said unto her "great is your faith." "Be it unto you as you wish." And the woman's daughter was healed immediately.[79] In the synagogue at Capernaum a man possessed by an unclean spirit said to Jesus "Let us alone . . . I know who you are, the Holy One of God." Jesus rebuked the unclean spirit, told it to come out of the man, and after crying with a loud voice it came out of the man.[80]

When blind Bartimaeus called out to Jesus and asked to receive his sight, Jesus said to him: "Go thy way; thy faith hath made thee whole." And immediately Bartimaeus received his sight.[81] When Jesus saw a man that had been born blind, Jesus spat on the ground, made clay of the spittle, anointed the eyes of the blind man with the clay, and told the blind man to go and wash in the pool of Siloam. The man went, washed and gained his sight. [82] When two blind men followed Jesus, asking him to have mercy on them that they might receive their sight, Jesus asked them if they believed he was able to heal them. They said yes, and then he touched their eyes and said, "according to your faith be it unto you." Immediately their eyes were opened. And Jesus told them not

---

[79] *See Matthew 15:22-28* (AMP)

[80] *See Mark 1:23-27*

[81] *See Mark 10:46-52*

[82] *See John 9:7*

to tell anyone.[83] When two blind men sitting by the road heard that Jesus was passing nearby, they called out for mercy. The crowd told them to be quiet, but the blind men continued to cry out for mercy. Jesus stopped and asked them what they wanted. They told him that they wanted their eyes opened. Jesus had compassion on them, touched their eyes and immediately they received their sight, and followed Jesus.[84]

A certain ruler, whose daughter was at home dead, came to Jesus and said, "come and lay thy hand upon her and she shall live." Jesus went to the ruler's house, took the girl by the hand, and she arose.[85] When Jesus came across the funeral procession of a widow burying her only son, he had compassion on the woman. Jesus touch the funeral bier and said, "Young man, I say unto thee, Arise." And the dead man sat up and began to speak.[86] When Jesus raised Lazarus from the dead, he cried out to Lazarus from outside of the cave in which Lazarus was buried. And Lazarus came out of the cave still bound hand and foot with graveclothes.[87]

Near the Sea of Galilee, the people brought Jesus a man who was deaf and had a speech impediment. Jesus took the man aside from the crowd, put his fingers into the man's

---

[83] *See Matthew 9:27-30*

[84] *See Matthew 20:30-34*

[85] *See Matthew 9:18-25*

[86] *See Luke 7:12-15*

[87] *See John 11:1-44*

ear, spit, touched the man's tongue, looked up to heaven, and said "be opened." And the man was completely healed. Jesus told the man to tell no one.[88] When Jesus came down from the Mount of Transfiguration a man asked him to heal his son that had a dumb spirit. Jesus rebuked the spirit and said, "Thou dumb and deaf spirit, I charge thee, come out of him, and enter no more into him." Then the spirit cried and came out of him. [89]

Sometimes Jesus spoke to the person with the illness, sometimes he spoke to the demon, sometimes he spoke to the person who came in faith on behalf of the diseased person; sometimes Jesus told the diseased person that their faith had made them whole, sometimes he touched the diseased person; sometimes he healed the person before the crowd; sometimes Jesus took the person away from the crowd and healed them privately; sometimes Jesus gave instructions to the person after he healed them; sometimes he gave no instructions at all; sometimes he told the healed person to go and tell others what God had done; sometimes he told the healed person to go and tell no one. God's provision for one person and their circumstances, is not the same for every person and their circumstances. Find out God's best for you and your circumstances by feeding your spirit on the Word of God.

My son, attend to my words; incline thine ear unto my sayings. Let them not depart from thine eyes; keep them

---

[88] *See Mark 7:31-36*

[89] *See Mark 9:16-25*

in the midst of thine heart. For they are life unto those that find them, and health to all their flesh. (Proverbs 4:20-22)

CHAPTER VII

HEAR FROM GOD

And there was a cloud that overshadowed them: and a voice came out of the cloud, saying, This is my beloved Son: hear him. (Mark 9:7)

{I}t is written, Man shall not live by bread along, but by every word that proceedeth out of the mouth of God. (Matthew 4:4)

The more we feed on the Word of God the more we will hear from God. Many Christians desire to hear more from God and hear from him on a deeper level. What the King James version of the Bible refers to as the deep things of God, the *Amplified Bible* refers to as "divine counsels and things hidden and beyond man's scrutiny."[90] To hear from God on a deeper level, we must grow in our understanding of God. The more we feed on the Word of God and put into practice what we know of the Word of God, the more we will grow in our understanding of God and hear from God on a deeper level.

> *And be sure to put into practice what you hear. The more you do this, the more you will understand what I tell you.* (*Mark 4:24*, TLB)

---

[90] I *Corinthians 2:10*

The Word of God is like a seed.[91] The more we hear and understand the Word of God, the more we become the good ground capable of bearing the thirty, sixty, and hundredfold return that the Bible promises.

> *[11] Now the parable is this: The seed is the Word of God. ... the good ground are those who, having heard the word with a noble and good heart, keep it and bear fruit with patience. (Luke 8:11-15, NKJV)*

> *But he that received seed into the good ground is he that heareth the word, and understandeth it; which also beareth fruit, and bringeth forth, some an hundredfold, some sixty, some thirty. (Matthew 13:23)*

The more we grow in our understanding of what God says, the more we will hear God speak to us on a deeper level and the more our lives will bear fruit. As in the parable of the talents where every man received in accordance with his individual ability,[92] God speaks to us on a level commensurate with our understanding.

> *With many such parables {Jesus} spoke the Word to them, as they were able to hear and to comprehend and understand.*
> *(Mark 4:33, AMP)*

---

[91] *See Luke 8:11-15*

[92] *See Matthew 25:15*

As Christians, we are repeatedly assured of our ability to hear from God.

> *My sheep hear my voice, and I know them, and they follow me. (John 10:27)*

> *He that is of God heareth God's words: . . . (John 8:47)*

Although God can speak to us audibly – the Bible is rife with examples - we don't need to hear an audible voice to hear God speak to us.

<u>God speaks to us through Jesus</u>

> *. . . {A}nd his name is called The Word of God. (Revelation 19:13)*

> *[1] In the past God spoke to our forefathers through the prophets at many times and in various ways, [2] but in these last days he has spoken to us by his Son, whom he appointed heir of all things, and through whom he made the universe. (Hebrews 1:1-2, NIV)*

Jesus and the Word of God are one. Because Jesus and the Word of God are one, when we read or hear the Word of God, we hear Jesus.

> *[1] In the beginning was the Word, and the Word was with God, and the Word was God. . .. [14] And the Word was made flesh, and dwelt among us, (and we beheld his glory, the glory as of the only begotten of the Father,) full of grace and truth. (John 1:1-14)*

Jesus and God are one.

> *[8] Philip saith unto him, Lord, shew us the Father, and it sufficeth us. [9] Jesus saith unto him, Have I been so long time with you, and yet hast thou not known me, Philip? He that hath seen me hath seen the Father; and how sayest thou then, Shew us the Father? (John 14:8-9)*

> *I and my Father are one. (John 10:30)*

Because Jesus and God are one, and Jesus only says what God says, when we hear Jesus, we hear God.

> *[10] {T}he words I say are not my own but are from my Father who lives in me. . . (John 14:10, TLB)*

Jesus is the key to every revelation of God and every promise from God.

> *For it pleased the Father that in him should all fulness dwell; (Colossians 1:19)*

> *For no matter how many promises God has made, they are "Yes" in Christ. . . . (II Corinthians 1:20, NIV)*

> *In whom are hid all the treasures of wisdom and knowledge. (II Colossians 2:3)*

> *[3] For as you know him better, he will give you, through his great power, everything you*

need for living a truly good life: he even shares his own glory and his own goodness with us! [4] And by that same mighty power he has given us all the other rich and wonderful blessings he promised; for instance, the promise to save us from the lust and rottenness all around us, and to give us his own character. (2 Peter 1:3-4, TLB)

[30] . . . Christ Jesus, who of God is made unto us wisdom, and righteousness, and sanctification, and redemption; [31] That, according as it is written, He that glorieth, let him glory in the Lord. (I Corinthians 1:30-31)

God speaks to us when we pray

[28] Father, glorify thy name. Then came there a voice from heaven, saying, I have both glorified it, and will glorify it again. [29] The people therefore, that stood by, and heard it, said that it thundered: others said, An angel spake to him. [30] Jesus answered and said, This voice came not because of me, but for your sakes. (John 12:28-30 NKJV)

God speaks to us through Angels

[26] {T}he angel Gabriel was sent from God unto a city of Galilee, named Nazareth, [27] To a virgin . . . and the virgin's name was Mary. . . . [30] And the angel said unto her, Fear not, Mary: for thou hast found favor with God. [31] And, behold, thou shalt conceive in thy womb, and bring forth a son, and shalt call his name JESUS. (Luke 1:26-31)

[15] {T}he Angel of the Lord called to Abraham a second time out of heaven, [16] and said: "By Myself I have sworn, says the Lord, because you have done this thing, and have not withheld your son, your only son - [17] blessing I will bless you, and multiplying I will multiply your descendants as the stars of the heaven and as the sand which is on the seashore; and your descendants shall possess the gate of their enemies. [18] In your seed all the nations of the earth shall be blessed, because you have obeyed My voice." (Genesis 22:15-18, NKJV)

[8] And there were in the same country shepherds abiding in the field . . . [9] And, lo, the angel of the Lord came upon them . . . [10] And the angel said unto them, Fear not: for, behold, I bring you good tidings of great joy, which shall be to all people. [11] For unto you is born this day in the city of David a Saviour, which is Christ the Lord. (Luke 2:8-11)

[12] And by the hands of the apostles were many signs and wonders wrought among the people; . . . [15] Insomuch that they brought forth the sick into the streets, and laid them on beds and on couches, that at the least the shadow of Peter passing by might overshadow some of them. [16] There came also a multitude out of the cities round about unto Jerusalem, bringing sick folks, and them which were vexed with unclean spirits: and they were healed everyone. [17] Then the high priest rose up, and all they that were with him, . . . [18] And they laid their hands on the apostles, and put them in the common prison. [19] But the angel of the Lord by night opened the prison doors, and brought them forth, and said, [20] Go, stand and speak in the temple to the people all the words of this life. (Acts 5:12-20)

The Revelation of Jesus Christ, which God gave unto him, to shew unto his servants things which must shortly come to pass; and he sent and signified it by his angel unto his servant John. (Revelation 1:1)

God speaks to us in dreams and visions.

[20] But while he thought on these things, behold, the angel of the Lord appeared unto him in a dream, saying Joseph, thou son of David, fear not to take unto thee Mary thy wife: for that which is conceived in her is of the Holy Ghost. [21] And she shall bring forth a son, and thou shalt call his name JESUS: (Matthew 1:20-21)

(11) And when they were come into the house, they saw the young child with Mary his mother, and fell down, and worshipped him: and when they had opened their treasures, they presented unto him gifts; gold, and frankincense, and myrrh. (12) And being warned of God in a dream that they should not return to Herod, they departed into their own country another way. (Matthew 2:11-12)

And when they were departed, behold, the angel of the Lord appeareth to Joseph in a dream, saying, Arise, and take the young child and his mother, and flee into Egypt, and be thou there until I bring thee word: for Herod will seek the young child to destroy him. (Matthew 2:13)

[19] But when Herod was dead, behold, an angel of the Lord appeareth in a dream to Joseph in Egypt, [20] Saying, Arise, and take the young child and his mother, and go into the land of Israel: for they are dead which

sought the young child's life.
(Matthew 2:19-20)

[10] And there was a certain disciple at Damascus, named Ananias; and to him said the Lord in a vision, Ananias . . . [11] Arise, and go into the street which is called Straight, and inquire in the house of Judas, for one called Saul, of Tarsus: for behold, he prayeth, [12] And hath seen in a vision a man named Ananias coming in, and putting his hand on him, that he might receive his sight. . . . [15] . . . Go thy way: for he is a chosen vessel unto me, to bear my name before the Gentiles, and kings, and the children of Israel:
(Acts 9:10-15)

[1] There was a certain man . . . called Cornelius, . . . [3] He saw in a vision . . . an angel of God coming in to him and saying unto him, Cornelius. [4] . . . Thy alms are come up for a memorial before God. [5] Now send men to Joppa, and call for one Simon, whose surname is Peter: [6] . . . he shall tell thee what thou oughtest to do. (Acts 10:1-6)[93]

[19] And a vision appeared to Paul in the night; There stood a man of Macedonia, and prayed him, saying, Come over into

---

[93] The obedience of Cornelius and Peter led to the Apostles and brethren understanding that Jesus lived, died, and was resurrected for all men.
(*See Acts 11:1-18; see also Acts 15:7-11*)

Macedonia, and help us. [10] And after he had seen the vision, immediately we endeavoured to go into Macedonia, assuredly gathering that the Lord had called us for to preach the gospel unto them. (Acts 16:9-10)

[9] Then spake the Lord to Paul in the night by a vision, Be not afraid, but speak, and hold not thy peace: [10] For I am with thee, and no man shall set on thee to hurt thee: for I have much people in this city. (Acts 18:9-10)

[17] And it came to pass, that, when I was come again to Jerusalem, even while I prayed in the temple, I was in a trance: [18] And saw him saying unto me, Make haste, and get thee quickly out of Jerusalem: for they will not receive thy testimony concerning me.. . .
[21] And he said unto me, Depart: for I will send thee far hence unto the Gentiles.
(Acts 22:17-21)

I will bless the Lord, Who has given me counsel; my heart also instructs me in the night seasons. (Psalms 16:7, NKJV)

God speaks to us through people

[14] How then shall they call on him in whom they have not believed? And how shall they believe in him of whom they have not heard? And how shall they hear without a preacher? [15] And how shall they preach, except they be sent? . . . (Romans 10:14-15)

> *And he said unto them, Go ye into all the world, and preach the gospel to every creature. (Mark 1:15)*

Jesus is living proof that God speaks to us through people. All of Jesus' earthly ministry - his teachings, miracles, death, and resurrection – until he returned to the Father following his crucifixion, was fulfilled as the Son of man.

> *Since we God's children, are human beings – made of flesh and blood – he became flesh and blood too by being born in human form . . . (Hebrews 2:14, TLB)*

> *. . . Jesus of Nazareth, a man approved of God among you by miracles and wonders and signs, which God did by him in the midst of you, as ye yourselves also know: (Acts 2:22)*

> *For there is one God, and one mediator between God and men, the man Christ Jesus; (I Timothy 2:5)*

Children of God, and messengers from God, hear from God and speak the Word of God through the Spirit of God.

> *For he whom God hath sent speaketh the words of God; for God giveth not the Spirit by measure unto him. (John 3:34)*

> *[17] And it shall come to pass in the last days, saith God, I will pour out of my Spirit upon all*

flesh: and your sons and your daughters shall prophesy, and your young men shall see visions, and your old men shall dream dreams: [18] And on my servants and on my handmaidens I will pour out in those days of my Spirit; and they shall prophesy: (Acts 2:17-18)

[3] But he that prophesieth speaketh unto men to, edification, and exhortation, and comfort. . . . [12] Even so ye, forasmuch as ye are zealous of spiritual gifts, seek that ye may excel to the edifying of the church. . . . [24] But if all prophesy, and there come in one that believeth not, or one unlearned, he is convinced of all, he is judged of all: [25] And thus are the secrets of his heart made manifest; and so falling down on his face he will worship God, and report that God is in you of a truth. (I Corinthians 14:3-24)

Our words are wise because they are from God, telling of God's wise plan to bring us into the glories of heaven. This plan was hidden in former times, though it was made for our benefit before the world began. (I Corinthians 2:7, TLB)

God speaks to us through the Holy Spirit

In olden times God did not share this plan with his people, but now he has revealed it by the Holy Spirit to his apostles and prophets. (Ephesians 3:5, TLB)

But the natural, nonspiritual man does not accept or welcome or admit into his heart the gifts and teachings and revelations of the Spirit of God, for they are folly {meaningless nonsense} to him; and he is incapable of knowing them {of progressively recognizing, understanding, and becoming better acquainted with them} because they are spiritually discerned and estimated and appreciated. (I Corinthians 2:14, AMP)

Howbeit when he, the Spirit of truth, is come, he will guide you into all truth: for he shall not speak of himself; but whatsoever he shall hear, that shall he speak: and he will shew you things to come. (John 16:13)

<u>God speaks to us through the Holy Spirit in us</u>

[38] He that believeth on me, as the scripture hath said, out of his belly shall flow rivers of living water. [39] (But this spake he of the Spirit, which they that believe on him should receive: for the Holy Ghost was not yet given; because that Jesus was not yet glorified.). (John 7:38-39)

What? Know ye not that your body is the temple of the Holy Ghost which is in you, which ye have of God, . . .
(I Corinthians 6:16)

[20] And are built upon the foundation of the apostles and prophets, Jesus Christ himself being the chief corner stone; [21] In whom all

the building fitly framed together growth unto an holy temple in the Lord; [22] In whom ye also are builded together for an inhabitation of God through the Spirit.
(Ephesians 2:20-22)

[11] For what person perceives {knows and understands} what passes through a man's thoughts except the man's own spirit within him? Just so no one discerns {comes to know and comprehend} the thoughts of God except the Spirit of God. [12] Now we have not received the spirit {that belongs to} the world, but the {Holy} Spirit Who is from God, {given to us} that we might realize and comprehend and appreciate the gifts {of divine favor and blessing so freely and lavishly} bestowed on us by God. (I Corinthians 2:11-12, AMP)

God speaks to us through the scriptures

[16] All scripture is given by inspiration of God, and is profitable for doctrine, for reproof, for correction, for instruction in righteousness; [17] That the man of God may be perfect, thoroughly furnished unto all good works. (II Timothy 3:16-17)

[30] And many other signs truly did Jesus in the presence of his disciples, which are not written in this book: [31] But these are written, that ye might believe that Jesus is the Christ, the Son of God; and that believing ye might have life through his name.
(John 20:30-31)

> *[25] Now to Him Who is able to strengthen you in the faith which is in accordance with my Gospel and the preaching of (concerning) Jesus Christ (the Messiah), according to the revelation (the unveiling) of the mystery of the plan of redemption which was kept in silence and secret for long ages. [26] But is now disclosed and through the prophetic Scriptures is made known to all nations, according to the command of the eternal God, [to win them] to obedience to the faith. (Romans 16:25-26, AMP)*

Jesus, read, taught about, relied on, quoted, and fulfilled the scriptures. When Jesus rebuked Satan in the wilderness, Jesus repeatedly said "It is written"[94] and relied on the scriptures to guide His behavior. When Jesus went into the synagogue at Nazareth, Jesus read and spoke to the people about what God has said in the scriptures.

> *[17] {A}nd when he had opened the book, he found the place where it was written [18] The Spirit of the Lord is upon me, because he hath anointed me to preach the gospel to the poor; he hath sent me to heal the brokenhearted, to preach deliverance to the captives, and recovering of sight to the blind, to set at liberty them that are bruised. [19] To preach the acceptable year of the Lord. [20] And he closed the book, and he gave it again to the minister, and sat down. . . . [21] And he began*

---

[94] *Matthew 4:1-10*

to say unto them, This day is this scripture fulfilled in your ears. (Luke 4:17-21)

Jesus revealed himself in and through the scriptures.

Search the scriptures; for in them ye think ye have eternal life: and they are they which testify of me. (John 5:39)

[44] And he said unto them, These are the words which I spake unto you, while I was yet with you, that all things must be fulfilled, which were written in the law of Moses, and in the prophets, and in the psalms, concerning me. [45] Then opened he their understanding, that they might understand the scriptures. [46] And said unto them, Thus it is written, and thus it behooved Christ to suffer, and to rise from the dead the third day: (Luke 24:44-46)

These things understood not his disciples at the first: but when Jesus was glorified, then remembered they that these things were written of him, and that they had done these things unto him. (John 12:16)

Before his crucifixion, Jesus explained that the things that had not yet happened, were already written in the scriptures.

. . . Behold, we go up to Jerusalem, and all things that are written by the prophets concerning the Son of man shall be accomplished. (Luke 18:31)

The Son of man goeth as it is written of him: but woe unto that man by whom the Son of man is betrayed! It had been good for that man if he had not been born. (Matthew 26:24)

[53] Thinkest thou that I cannot now pray to my Father, and he shall presently give me more than twelve legions of angels. [54] But how then shall the scriptures be fulfilled, that thus it must be. (Matthew 26:53-54)

*But all this was done, that the scriptures of the prophets might be fulfilled. . . .
(Matthew 26:56)*

God does speak to us audibly, and those with spiritual ears to hear will hear

[31] When Moses saw it, he wondered at the sight: and as he drew near to behold it, the voice of the Lord came unto him, [32] Saying, I am the God of thy fathers, . . . [33] Then said the Lord to him, Put off thy shoes from thy feet: for the place whither thou standest is holy ground. [34] I have seen, I have seen the affliction of my people which is in Egypt, and I have heard their groaning, and am come down to deliver them. And now come, I will send thee into Egypt. (Acts 7:31-34)

[4] . . . Saul, Saul, why persecutest thou me? [5] And he said, Who art thou, Lord? And the Lord said, I am Jesus whom thou persecutest: it is hard for thee to kick against the pricks.

[6] And he trembling and astonished said, Lord, what wilt thou have me to do? And the Lord said unto him, Arise, and go into the city, and it shall be told thee what thou must do.
[7] And the men which journeyed with him stood speechless, hearing a voice, but seeing no man. (Act 9:4-7)

[15] And I said, Who art thou, Lord? And he said, I am Jesus whom thou persecutest.
[16] But rise, and stand upon thy feet: for I have appeared unto thee for this purpose, to make thee a minister and a witness both of these things which thou has seen, and of those things in which I will appear unto thee;
[17] Delivering thee from the people, and from the Gentiles, unto whom now I send thee,
[18] To open their eyes, and to turn them from darkness to light, and from the power of Satan unto God, that they may receive forgiveness of sins and inheritance among them which are sanctified by faith that is in me.
(Acts 26:15-18)

[5] But who could possibly fight and win this battle except by believing that Jesus is truly the Son of God? [6-8] And we know he is, because God said so with a voice from heaven when Jesus was baptized, and again as he was facing death – yes, not only at his baptism but also as he faced death. And the Holy Spirit, forever truthful, says it too. So we have these three witnesses: the voice of the Holy Spirit in our hearts, the voice from heaven at Christ's baptism, and the voice before he died. And

they all say the same thing: that Jesus Christ is the Son of God. (1 John 5:5-8, TLB)

Hearing from God is a choice

[39] She had a sister called Mary, which also sat at Jesus' feet, and heard his word. [40] But Martha was cumbered about much serving, and came to him, and said, Lord, dost thou not care that my sister hath left me to serve alone? Bid her therefore that she help me. [41] And Jesus answered and said unto her, Martha, Martha, though art careful and troubled about many things: [42] But one thing is needful: and Mary hath chosen that good part . . . (Luke 10:39-42)

We can hear God speak to us even before we are born again.

[11] And when the Pharisees saw it, they said unto his disciples, Why eateth your Master with publicans and sinners? [12] But when Jesus heard that, he said unto them, They that be whole need not a physician, but they that are sick. [13] But go ye and learn what that meaneth, I will have mercy, and not sacrifice: for I am not come to call the righteous, but sinners to repentance. (Matthew 9:11-13)

But whether we hear, believe and heed his voice is our choice.

But now is the time. Never forget the warning, "Today if you hear God's voice speaking to

> *you, do not harden your hearts against him, as the people of Israel did when they rebelled against him in the desert." (Hebrews 3:15, TLB)*
>
> *So see to it that you do not reject Him or refuse to listen to and heed Him Who is speaking {to you now}. For if they {the Israelites} did not escape when they refused to listen and heed Him Who warned and divinely instructed them {here} on earth {revealing with heavenly warnings His will}, how much less shall we escape if we reject and turn our backs on Him Who cautions and admonishes {us} from heaven? (Hebrews 12:25, AMP)*
>
> *Behold, I stand at the door, and knock: if any man hear my voice, and open the door, I will come in to him, and will sup with him, and he with me. (Revelation 3:20)*

Hearing is a prerequisite for believing. Believing is a prerequisite for trusting. And trusting is evidenced by faith.

> *How then shall they call on him in whom they have not believed? And how shall they believe in him of whom they have not heard? . . . (Romans 10:14)*
>
> *[18] And to whom sware he that they should not enter into his rest, but to them that believed not? [19] So we see that they could not enter in because of unbelief. (Hebrews 3:18-19)*

For unto us was the gospel preached, as well as unto them: but the word preached did not profit them, not being mixed with faith in them that heard it. (Hebrews 4:2)

But without faith is it impossible to please him: for he that cometh to God must believe that he is, and that he is a rewarder of them that diligently seek him. (Hebrews 11:6)

Jesus said those who hear him but ignore what he says are foolish, and those who hear him and follow what he says are wise.

[24] All who listen to my instructions and follow them are wise, like a man who builds his house on solid rock. . .. [26] But those who hear my instructions and ignore them are foolish, like a man who builds his house on sand. (Matthew 7:24-26, TLB)

When we choose to hear and believe God, he will tell us things to come.

{Prompted} by faith Noah, being forewarned by God concerning events of which as yet there was no visible sign, took heed and diligently and reverently constructed and prepared an ark for the deliverance of his own family. . . . (Hebrews 11:7, AMP)

[25] And, behold, there was a man in Jerusalem, whose name was Simeon; and the same man was just and devout, waiting for the consolation of Israel: and the Holy Ghost was

upon him. [26] And it was revealed unto him by the Holy Ghost, that he should not see death, before he had seen the Lord's Christ. (Luke 2:25-26)

[27] The Holy Spirit had impelled him {Simeon} to go to the Temple that day; and so, when Mary and Joseph arrived to present the baby Jesus to the Lord in obedience to the law, Simeon was there and took the child in his arms, praising God. [29 – 31] "Lord," he said, "now I can die content! For I have seen him as you promised me I would. I have seen the Savior you have given to the world. (Luke 2:27-32, TLB)

When we choose to hear and believe God, he will speak for us and through us.

[19] But when they deliver you up, take no thought how or what ye shall speak: for it shall be given you in that same hour what ye shall speak. [20] For it is not ye that speak but the Spirit of your Father which speaketh in you. (Matthew 10:19-20)

For I will give you a mouth and wisdom, which all your adversaries shall not be able to gainsay nor resist. (Luke 21:15)

Likewise the Spirit also helpeth our infirmities: for we know not what we should pray for as we ought: but the Spirit itself maketh intercession for us with groanings which cannot be uttered. (Romans 8:26)

When we choose to hear and believe God, we will walk in the provision of God.

> *The thief's purpose is to steal, kill and destroy. My purpose is to give life in all its fullness. (John 10:10, TLB)*

In the first biblically recorded miracle attributed to Jesus, he turned water into wine for a wedding feast.

> *[5] His mother saith unto the servants, Whatsoever he saith unto you, do it. . . . [7] Jesus saith unto them, Fill the waterpots with water. And they filled them up to the brim. [8] And he saith unto them, Draw out now, and bear unto the governor of the feast. . . . [9] When the ruler of the feast had tasted the water that was made wine, and knew not whence it was: (but the servants which drew the water knew;) the governor of the feast called the bridegroom, [10] And he saith unto him, Every man at the beginning doth set forth good wine; and when men have well drunk, then that which is worse: but thou hast kept the good wine until now. (John 2:5-10)*

In one of Peter's earliest interactions with Jesus, when Peter heeded the Word of God, Peter immediately went from toiling all night and catching nothing, to overabundance.

> *[3] Then He got into one of the boats, which was Simon's, and asked him to put out a little from the land. And He sat down and taught the multitudes from the boat. [4] When He*

had stopped speaking, He said to Simon, "Launch out into the deep and let down your nets for a catch." [5] But Simon answered and said to Him, "Master, we have toiled all night and caught nothing; nevertheless at Your word I will let down the net." [6] And when they had done this, they caught a great number of fish, and their net was breaking. [7] So they signaled to their partners in the other boat to come and help them. And they came and filled both the boats so that they began to sink. (Luke 5:3-7, NKJV)

In one of Peter's latest interactions with Jesus, when Peter heeded the Word of God, Peter again immediately went from toiling all night and catching nothing, to overabundance.

*[3] Simon Peter saith unto them, I go a fishing. They say unto him, We also go with thee. They went forth, and entered into a ship immediately; and that night they caught nothing. [4] But when the morning was now come, Jesus stood on the shore: but the disciples knew not that it was Jesus. [5] Then Jesus saith unto them, Children, have ye any meat? They answered him, No. [6] And he said unto them, Cast the net on the right side of the ship, and ye shall find. They cast therefore, and now they were not able to draw it for the multitude of fishes.
(John 21:3-6)*

When we choose to hear and believe God, we will walk in the wisdom and power of God.

> *[24] But unto them which are called, both Jews and Greeks, Christ the power of God, and the wisdom of God. [25] Because the foolishness of God is wiser than men, and the weakness of God is stronger than men. (I Corinthians 1:24-25)*

> *[4] I thank my God always on your behalf, for the grace of God which is given you by Jesus Christ; [5] That in every thing ye are enriched by him, in all utterance, and in all knowledge. (I Corinthians 1:4-5)*

In whatever manner we hear from God, the more we feed on God's word the more our external life will evidence his internal presence.

> *[11] Now the parable is this: The seed is the Word of God. ... the good ground are those who . . . having heard the word with a noble and good heart, keep it and bear fruit with patience. (Luke 8:11-15, NKJV)*

> *[3] And he spake many things unto them in parables, saying, Behold, a sower went forth to sow; [4] And when he sowed, some seeds fell by the way side, . . . [8] But other fell into good ground, and brought forth fruit, some an hundredfold, some sixtyfold, some thirtyfold. [9] Who hath ears to hear, let him hear. (Matthews 13:3-8)*

{T}he dumb ass speaking with man's voice forbad the madness of the prophet. (2 Peter 2:16)

CHAPTER VIII

ONLY SAY WHAT GOD SAYS

The word "followers" in the Greek means to imitate. We are to imitate God as a child does his father. If a child imitates his father, he will walk like him, talk like him, and pattern his every move after him. - Charles Capp[95]

Be ye therefore followers of God, as dear children; (Ephesians 5:1)

The Power of the Tongue

> *If any man offend not in word, the same is a perfect man, and able also to bridle the whole body. (James 3:2)*

> *Be ye therefore perfect, even as your Father which is in heaven is perfect. (Matthew 5:48)*

The power that results in death, life, fear, faith, poverty, and abundance resides in our heart, and is made manifest in our life, by what comes out of our mouth.

> *Death and life are in the power of the tongue... (Proverbs 18:21, NKJV)*

---

95 *The Tongue, A Creative Force*

> *Even so the tongue is a little member, and boasteth great things. Behold, how great a matter a little fire kindleth! [6] And the tongue is a fire, a world of iniquity: so is the tongue among our members, that it defileth the whole body, and setteth on fire the course of nature: and it is set on fire of hell. (James 3:5-6)*

> *For he that will love life, and see good days, let him refrain his tongue from evil, and his lips that they speak no guile: (1 Peter 3:10)*

Every word we speak creates. Either for good, or for ill. Everything we say is either an evil report that leads to death, fear, and poverty. Or a good report that leads to life, faith, and abundance.

> *Out of the same mouth proceedeth blessing and cursing. My brethren, these things ought not so to be. (James 3:10)*

Everything we say that is inconsistent with the Word of God, is an evil report that leads to death, fear, and poverty.

> *[7] And the Lord said: "I have surely seen the oppression of My people who are in Egypt, and have heard their cry because of their taskmasters, for I know their sorrows. [8] So I have come down to deliver them out of the hand of the Egyptians, and to bring them from that land to a good and large land, to a land flowing with milk and honey, to the place of the Canaanites and the Hittites and the Amorites and the Perizzites and the Hivites and the Jebusites. (Exodus 3:7-8, NKJV)*

[21] And I will give this people favor in the sight of the Egyptians; and it shall be, when you go, that you shall not go empty-handed. [22] But every woman shall ask of her neighbor, namely, of her who dwells near her house, articles of silver, articles of gold, and clothing; and you shall put them on your sons and on your daughters. So you shall plunder the Egyptians." (Exodus 3:21-22, NKJV)

[29] Then Moses and Aaron went and gathered together all the elders of the children of Israel. [30] And Aaron spoke all the words which the Lord had spoken to Moses. . . . [31] So the people believed; . . . (Exodus 4:29-31, NKJV)

[35] Now the children of Israel had done according to the word of Moses, and they had asked from the Egyptians articles of silver, articles of gold, and clothing. [36] And the Lord had given the people favor in the sight of the Egyptians, so that they granted them what they requested. Thus they plundered the Egyptians. [37] Then the children of Israel journeyed from Rameses to Succoth, about six hundred thousand men on foot, beside children. [38] A mixed multitude went up with them also, and flocks and herds – a great deal of livestock. (Exodus 12:35-38, NKJV)

And the Lord hardened the heart of Pharaoh king of Egypt, and he pursued the children of Israel; . . . (Exodus 14:8, NKJV)

[21] Then Moses stretched out his hand over the sea; and the Lord caused the sea to go back by a strong east wind all that night, and made the sea into dry land, and the waters were divided. [22] So the children of Israel went into the midst of the sea on dry ground, and the waters were a wall to them on their right hand and on their left. [23] And the Egyptians pursued and went after them into the midst of the sea, all Pharaoh's horses, his chariots, and his horsemen.
(Exodus 14:21-23, NKJV)

[28] Then the waters returned and covered the chariots, the horsemen, and all the army of Pharaoh that came into the sea after them. Not so much as one of them remained.
[29] But the children of Israel had walked on dry land in the midst of the sea, and the waters were a wall to them on their right hand and on their left. (Exodus 14:28-29, NKJV)

Thus Israel saw the great work which the Lord had done in Egypt; so the people feared the Lord, and believed the Lord and His servant Moses. (Exodus 14:31, NKJV)

[1] And the Lord spoke to Moses, saying,
[2] "Send men to spy out the land of Canaan, which I am giving to the children of Israel; from each tribe of their fathers you shall send a man, every one a leader among them."
(Numbers 13:1-2, NKJV)

[26] Now they departed and came back to Moses, and Aaron and all the congregation of the children of Israel . . . [27] Then they told him, and said: "We went to the land where you sent us. It truly flows with milk and honey, and this is its fruit. . . ." [30] Then Caleb quieted the people before Moses, and said, "Let us go up at once and take possession, for we are well able to overcome it." [31] But the men who had gone up with him said, "We are not able to go up against the people, for they are stronger than we." [32] And they gave the children of Israel a bad report of the land which they had spied out . . .
(Numbers 13:26-32, NKJV)

[6] But Joshua the son of Nun and Caleb the son of Jephunneh, who were among those who had spied out the land, tore their clothes; and they spoke to all the congregation of the children of Israel, saying: "The land we passed through to spy out is an exceedingly good land. If the Lord delights in us, then He will bring us into this land and give it to us, 'a land which flows with milk and honey.' Only do not rebel against the Lord, nor fear the people of the land, for they are our bread; their protection has departed from them, and the Lord is with us. Do not fear them." And all the congregation said to stone them with stones. (Numbers 14:6-10, NKJV)

[11] Then the Lord said to Moses: "How long will these people reject Me? And how long will they not believe Me, with all the signs

> *which I have performed among them? . . . [23]. . . they certainly shall not see the land which I swore to their fathers, nor shall any of those who rejected Me see. [24] But My servant Caleb, because he has a different spirit in him and has followed Me fully, I will bring into the land where he went, and his descendants shall inherit it. . . . (Numbers 14:11-24 NKNV)*
>
> *[30] Except for Caleb the son of Jephunneh and Joshua the son of Nun, you shall by no means enter the land which I swore I would make you dwell in. (Numbers 14:30, NKJV)*
>
> *[36] Now the men whom Moses sent to spy out the land, who returned and made all the congregation complain against him by bringing a bad report of the land, those very men who brought the evil report about the land, died by the plague before the Lord. [38] But Joshua the son of Nun and Caleb the son of Jephunneh remained alive, of the men who went to spy out the land. (Number 14:36-38, NKJV)*

Joshua and Caleb received the same promises from God as the other ten leaders. Joshua and Caleb saw the same miracles performed by God, when he brought the Israelites out of Egypt, as the other ten leaders. Joshua and Caleb spied out the promised land at the same time with the other ten leaders. Joshua and Caleb saw the same inhabitants in the promised land as the other ten leaders. And Joshua and Caleb brought back the fruit from the promised land at the same time with the other ten leaders. But Joshua and Caleb brought back a different report than the other ten leaders. The ten leaders brought back a bad report, an evil report. Joshua and Caleb brought back a different report, a good report. They brought back a different report than the other ten leaders because they had a different spirit than the other ten leaders. Joshua and Caleb had the spirit of faith.

> *[6] Then the children of Judah came to Joshua in Gilgal. And Caleb the son of Jephunneh the Kenizzite said to him: "You know the word which the Lord said to Moses the man of God concerning you and me in Kadesh Barnea. [7] I was forty years old when Moses the servant of the Lord sent me from Kadesh Barnea to spy out the land, and I brought back word to him as it was in my heart. (Joshua 14:6-7, NKJV)*

> *A good man out of the good treasure of his heart bringeth forth that which is good; and an evil man out of the evil treasure of his heart bringeth forth that which is evil: for of the abundance of the heart his mouth speaketh. (Luke 6:45)*

Everything we say with the spirit of faith will be a good report that is consistent with the Word of God.

> *We having the same spirit of faith, according as it is written, I believed, and therefore have I spoken; we also believe, and therefore speak. (II Corinthians 4:13)*

The words that come out of our mouths are seeds that produce after their own kind. Every good report is consistent with the Word of God and produces life, faith, and abundance.

> *This Book of the Law shall not depart out of your mouth, but you shall meditate on it day and night, that you may observe and do according to all that is written in it. For then you shall make your way prosperous, and then you shall deal wisely and have good success. (Joshua 1:8, AMP)*

> *Be not deceived; God is not mocked: for whatsoever a man soweth, that shall he also reap. (Galatians 6:7)*

> *Let no corrupt communication proceed out of your mouth, but that which is good to the use of edifying, that it may minister grace unto the hearers. (Ephesians 4:29)*

The Heart and the Tongue

The heart and the tongue are inextricably linked. What goes into our heart determines what comes out of our mouth.

> *[18] But those things which proceed out of the mouth come forth from the heart; and they defile the man. [19] For out of the heart proceed evil thoughts, murders, adulteries, fornications, thefts, false witness, blasphemies; [20] These are the things which defile a man: . . . (Matthew 15:18-19)*

[34] O generation of vipers, how can ye, being evil, speak good things? For out of the abundance of the heart the mouth speaketh. [35] A good man out of the good treasure of the heart bringeth forth good things: and an evil man out of the evil treasure bringeth forth evil things. (Matthew 12:34-35)

The heart of the wise teaches his mouth, and addeth learning to his lips. (Proverbs 16:23)

And what comes out of our mouth determines our destiny.

[2] A man shall eat well by the fruit of his mouth, But the soul of the unfaithful feeds on violence. [3] He who guards his mouth preserves his life, But he who opens wide his lips shall have destruction. (Proverbs 13:2-3, NKJV)

The wicked is snared by the transgression of his lips, but the just will come out of trouble. (Proverbs 12:13, NKJV)

A fool's talk brings a rod to his back, but the lips of the wise protect them. (Proverbs 14:3, NIV)

The cornerstone to control of our destiny is control of what we let into our heart.

Keep your heart with all diligence, for out of it spring the issues of life. (Proverbs 4:23, NKJV)

And here again, as always, Jehovah-Jireh the Lord God our provider did not leave us helpless.

> *{F}or God's love has been poured out in our hearts through the Holy Spirit Who has been given to us. (Romans 5:5, AMP)*
>
> *[5] Trust in the Lord with all thine heart, and lean not on your own understanding; [6] In all thy ways acknowledge Him, and He shall direct thy paths. (Proverbs 3:5-6)*
>
> *[4] Abide in me, and I in you. As the branch cannot bear fruit of itself, except it abide in the vine, no more can ye, except ye abide in me. [5] I am the vine, ye are the branches: He that abideth in me and I in him, the same bringeth forth much fruit: for without me ye can do nothing. [6] If a man abide not in me, he is cast forth as a branch, and is withered; and men gather them and cast them into the fire, and they are burned. [7] If ye abide in me, and my words abide in you, ye shall ask what ye will, and it shall be done unto you. (John 15:4-7)*

Offend Not in Word

> *[2] Wherein in time past ye walked according to the course of this world, according to the prince of the power of the air, the spirit that now worketh in the children of disobedience: [3] Among whom also we all had our conversation in times past in the lusts of the*

> *flesh, fulfilling the desires of the flesh and of the mind; and were by nature the children of wrath, even as others. (Ephesians 2:2-3)*

> *[22] . . . {P}ut off concerning the former conversation the old man, which is corrupt according to the deceitful lusts; [23] And be renewed in the spirit of your mind; [24] And that ye put on the new man, which after God is created in righteousness and true holiness. [25] Wherefore putting away lying, speak every man truth with his neighbor: for we are members one of another. (Ephesians 4:22-25)*

> *Let all bitterness, and wrath, and anger, and clamour, and evil speaking, be put away from you, with all malice: (Ephesians 4:31)*

> *Only let your conversation be as it becometh the gospel of Christ: That whether I come and see you, or else be absent, I may hear of your affairs, that ye stand fast in one spirit, with one mind striving together for the faith of the gospel; (Philippians 1:27)*

> *But as he which hath called you is holy, so be ye holy in all manner of conversation; (I Peter 1:15)*

As Christians, we are children of God and joint heirs with Christ.

> *[8] So then they that are in the flesh cannot please God. [9] But ye are not in the flesh, but in the Spirit, if so be that the Spirit of God*

> *dwell in you. Now if any have not the Spirit of Christ, he is none of his. . . [14] for as many as are led by the Spirit of God, they are the sons of God. [15] For ye have not received the spirit of bondage again to fear; but ye have received the Spirit of adoption, whereby we cry, Abba, Father. [16] The Spirit itself beareth witness with our spirit, that we are the children of God; [17] And if children then heirs; heirs of God, and joint-heirs with Christ; . . . [29] For whom he did foreknow he also did predestinate to be conformed to the image of his Son, that he might be the firstborn among many brethren. (Romans 8:8-29)*

So, although the tongue can be tamed by no man,[96] as children of God we can do all things through Jesus.

> *I can do all things through Christ which strengtheneth me. (Philippians 4:13)*

> *{F}or One is your Teacher, the Christ, and you are all brethren. (Matthew 23:8, NKJV)*

> *Ye call me Master and Lord: and ye say well; for so I am. (John 13:13)*

---

[96] *But the human tongue can be tamed by no man. It is a restless (undisciplined, irreconcilable) evil, full of deadly poison. (James 3:8 AMP)*

The disciple is not above his master: but every one that is perfect shall be as his master. (Luke 6:40)

Because we have the same Spirit as Jesus, we can walk as Jesus walked and talk as Jesus talked.

[1] Be ye therefore followers of God, as dear children; [2] And walk in love, as Christ also hath loved us, and hath given himself for us an offering and sacrifice to God for a sweet smelling savour. [3] But fornication, and all uncleanness, or covetousness, let it not be once named among you, as becometh saints; [4] Neither filthiness, nor foolish talking, nor jesting, which are not convenient: but rather giving of thanks. (Ephesians 5:1-4)

[8] For ye were sometimes darkness, but now are ye light in the Lord: walk as children of light: [9] {For the fruit of the Spirit is in all goodness and righteousness and truth}; (Ephesians 5:8-9)

As followers of Jesus, we should do what he does . . .

He that saith he abideth in him ought himself also so to walk, even as he walked. (I John 2:6)

. . . and say what He says.

What I tell you in darkness, that speak ye in light: and what ye hear in the ear, that preach ye upon the housetops. (Matthew 10:27)

The words of God have creative power, and Jesus is the Word of God made flesh.

> *In the beginning was the Word, and the Word was with God, and the Word was God. (John 1:1)*

> *Through faith we understand that the worlds were framed by the Word of God, so that things which are seen were not made of things which do appear. (Hebrews 11:3)*

> *[2] The earth was without form, and void; and darkness was on the face of the deep. And the Spirit of God was hovering over the face of the waters. [3] Then God said, "Let there be light"; and there was light. (Genesis 1:2-3, NKJV)*

We were created in the image of God, conformed to the image of his Son, and filled with the Holy Spirit. The same creative power that spoke the heavens and the earth into existence, created us, resides in us, and is available to us.

> *So God created man in his own image, in the image of God created he him; male and female created he them. (Genesis 1:27)*

> *For whom he did foreknow he also did predestinate to be conformed to the image of his Son, that he might be the firstborn among many brethren. (Romans 8:29)*

And though we separated from God through sin, God redeemed us to himself through grace.

> *[5] Having predestinated us unto the adoption of children by Jesus Christ to himself, according to the good pleasure of his will, [6] to the praise of the glory of his grace, wherein he hath made us accepted in the beloved. [7] In whom we have redemption through his blood, the forgiveness of sins, according to the riches of his grace; (Ephesians 1:5-7)*

And through his grace we became new creatures. Our spirits were born again, we were reconciled to God, and now have the power of God within us at our disposal.

> *[13] But now in Christ Jesus ye who sometimes were far off are made nigh by the blood of Christ. . . . [22] In whom ye also are builded together for an habitation of God through the Spirit. (Ephesians 2:13-22)*

> *[17] Therefore if any man be in Christ, he is a new creature: old things are passed away; behold, all things are become new. [18] And all things are of God who hath reconciled us to himself by Jesus Christ and hath given to us the ministry of reconciliation: (II Corinthians 5:17-18)*

> *I can do all things through Christ which strengtheneth me. (Philippians 4:13)*

Because we have been recreated in the image of God and the Spirit of God resides within us, our words have creative power.

> *[12] And on the morrow, when they were come from Bethany, he was hungry; [13] And seeing a fig tree afar off having leaves, he came, if haply he might find any thing thereon: and when he came to it, he found nothing but leaves; for the time of figs was not yet. [14] And Jesus answered and said unto it, No man eat fruit of thee hereafter for ever. And his disciples heard it. (Mark 11:12-14)*
>
> *[20] And in the morning, as they passed by, they saw the fig tree dried up from the roots. [21] And Peter calling to remembrance saith unto him, Master, behold, the fig tree which thou cursedst is withered away. [22] And Jesus answering saith unto them, Have faith in God. [23] For verily I say unto you That whosoever shall say unto this mountain, Be thou removed, and be thou cast into the sea; and shall not doubt in his heart, but shall believe that those things which he saith shall come to pass; he shall have whatsoever he saith. (Mark 11:20-21)*

Jesus, our example, was intentional in everything that he said. So, we should be intentional in everything that we say. In fact, Jesus cautioned against speaking idle words.

> *[36] But I say unto you, That every idle word that men shall speak, they shall give account thereof in the day of judgment. [37] For by thy*

> *words thou shalt be justified, and by thy words thou shalt be condemned. (Matthew 12:36-37)*

Jesus and the Holy Spirit are consistent. They only say what God has said, or what God has told them to say.

> *Howbeit when he, the Spirit of truth, is come, he will guide you into all truth: for he shall not speak of himself; but whatsoever he shall hear, that shall he speak: . . . (John 16:13)*

> *. . . The words I say are not my own but are from my Father who lives in me. (John 14:10, TLB)*

> *I could condemn you for much and teach you much, but I won't, for I say only what I am told to by the one who sent me; and he is Truth. (John 8:26, TLB)*

> *[49] For I have not spoken on My own authority; but the Father who sent Me gave Me a command, what I should say and what I should speak. [50] And I know that his command is everlasting life. Therefore, whatever I speak, just as the Father has told Me, so I speak. (John 12:49-50, NKJV)*

When we say what God has taught us to say, when we say what we've heard Jesus say, it pleases God.

> *[28] Then said Jesus unto them, When ye have lifted up the Son of man, then shall ye know that I am he, and that I do nothing of myself; but as my Father hath taught me, I speak these*

> *things. [29] . . . for I always do those things that please him. (John 8:28-29)*

Jesus has given us the words that God gave him.

> *For I have given unto them the words which thou gavest me: and they have received them, . . . (John 17:8)*

We can speak the words of God that Jesus spoke. We can please God as Jesus pleased God. We can be perfect, as Jesus is perfect. And we can speak words full of authority, power and love as the words spoken by Jesus are full of authority, power, grace and love.

> *For the Word of God is quick, and powerful, and sharper than any two-edged sword . . . (Hebrews 4:12)*

> *[31] And {Jesus} came down to Capernaum, a city of Galilee, and taught them on the sabbath days. [32] And they were astonished at his doctrine: for his word was with power. (Luke 4:31-32)*

> *[33] And in the synagogue there was a man, which had a spirit of an unclean devil, and cried out with a loud voice, [34] Saying, Let us alone; what have we to do with thee, thou Jesus of Nazareth? Art thou come to destroy us? I know thee who thou art; the Holy One of God. [35] And Jesus rebuked him, saying, Hold thy peace, and come out of him, And when the devil had thrown him in the midst, he came out of him, and hurt him not. [36] And*

> *they were all amazed, and spake among themselves, saying, What a word is this! For with authority and power he commandeth the unclean spirits, and they come out. (Luke 4:33-36)*

> *And all bare him witness, and wondered at the gracious words which proceeded out of his mouth. And they said, is not this Joseph's son? (Luke 4:22)*

Everything in the Bible is for our edification.

> *For whatever things were written aforetime were written for our learning, that we through patience and comfort of the scriptures might have hope. (Romans 15:4)*

And in the Bible, those who said what Jesus said walked in the wisdom and the power of Jesus.

> *[1] And I, brethren, when I came to you, came not with excellency of speech or of wisdom, declaring unto you the testimony of God. [2] For I determined not to know anything among you, save Jesus Christ, and him crucified. . .. [4] And my speech and my preaching was not with enticing words of man's wisdom, but in demonstration of the Spirit and of power. [5] That your faith should not stand in the wisdom of men, but in the power of God. (I Corinthians 2:4-5)*

When the disciples spoke as the spirit gave utterance, every man heard as every man needed to hear.

> *[4] And they were all filled with the Holy Ghost, and began to speak with other tongues, as the Spirit gave them utterance. [5] And there were dwelling at Jerusalem Jews, devout men, out of every nation under heaven. [6] Now when this was noised abroad, the multitude came together, and were confounded, because that every man heard them speak in his own language. (Acts 2:4-6)*

When the scribe echoed the words of Jesus, Jesus told the scribe he was not far from the kingdom of God.

> *[29] And Jesus answered him, The first of all commandments is, Hear, O Israel; The Lord our God is one Lord: [30] And thou shalt love the Lord thy God with all thy heart, and with all thy soul, and with all thy mind, and with all thy strength: this is the first commandment. [31] And the second is like, namely this, Thou shalt love thy neighbour as thyself. There is none other commandment greater than these. [32] And the scribe said unto him, Well, Master, thou hast said the truth: for there is one God; and there is none other but he: [33] And to love him with all the heart, and with all the understanding, and with all the soul, and with all the strength, and to love his neighbour as himself, is more than all whole burnt offerings and sacrifices. [34] And when Jesus saw that he answered discreetly, he said unto him, Thou art not far from the kingdom of God. ... (Mark 12:29-34)*

When the disciples said what Jesus told them to say, they received the results that Jesus said they would receive.

> *[2] And saith unto them, Go your way into the village over against you: and as soon as ye be entered into it, ye shall find a colt tied, whereon never man sat; loose him, and bring him. [3] And if any man say unto you, Why do ye this? Say ye that the Lord hath need of him; and straightway he will send him hither.*
> *[4] And they went their way, and found the colt tied by the door without in a place where two ways met; and they loose him. [5] And certain of them that stood there said unto them, What do ye, loosing the colt? [6] And they said unto them even as Jesus had commanded: and they let them go.*
> *(Mark 11:2-6)*

Jesus healed the sick with his word. We can do the same.

> *[16] When the even was come, they brought unto him many that were possessed with devils: and he cast out the spirits with his word, and healed all that were sick: [17] That it might be fulfilled which was spoken by Esaias the prophet, saying, Himself took our infirmities, and bare our sicknesses.*
> *(Matthew 8:16-17)*

> *[17] And these signs shall follow them that believe; In my name shall they cast out devils; they shall speak with new tongues; [18] They shall take up serpents; and if they drink any*

> *deadly thing, it shall not hurt them; they shall lay hands on the sick, and they shall recover. (Mark 16:17-18)*

Jesus overcame temptations with his words. We can do the same.

> *[1] Then was Jesus led up of the Spirit into the wilderness to be tempted of the devil. [2] And when he had fasted forty days and forty nights, he was afterward an hungred. [3] And when the tempter came to him, he said, If thou be the Son of God, command that these stones be made bread. [4] But he answered and said, It is written, Man shall not live by bread alone, but by every word that proceedeth out of the mouth of God. [5] Then the devil taketh him up into the holy city, and setteth him on a pinnacle of the temple, [6] And saith unto him, If thou be the Son of God, cast thyself down: for it is written, He shall give his angels charge concerning thee: and in their hands they shall bear thee up, lest at any time thou dash thy foot against a stone. [7] Jesus said unto him, It is written again, Thou shalt not tempt the Lord thy God. [8] Again, the devil taketh him up into an exceeding high mountain, and sheweth him all the kingdoms of the world, and the glory of them; [9] And saith unto him, All these things will I give thee, if thou wilt fall down and worship me. [10] Then saith Jesus unto him, Get thee hence, Satan: for it is written, Thou shalt worship the Lord thy God, and him only shalt thou serve. [11] Then the devil leaveth him,*

> *and, behold, angels came and ministered unto him. (Matthew 4:1-11)*

Jesus calmed the raging storm with his words. We can do the same.

> *[23] But as they sailed he fell asleep: and there came down a storm of wind on the lake; and they were filled with water, and were in jeopardy. [24] And they came to him, and awoke him, saying, Master, master, we perish. Then he arose, and rebuked the wind and the raging of the water: and they ceased, and there was calm. [25] And he said unto them, Where is your faith? And they being afraid wondered, saying one to another, What manner of man is this! For he commandeth even the winds and water, and they obey him. (Luke 8:23-25)*

> *[22] And Jesus answering saith to them, 'Have faith of God; [23] for verily I say to you, that whoever may say to this mount, Be taken up, and be cast into the sea, and may not doubt in his heart, but may believe that the things that he saith do come to pass, it shall be to him whatever he may say. [24] Because of this I say to you, all whatever – praying – ye do ask, believe that ye receive, and it shall be to you. (Mark 11:22-24, Young's Literal Translation of the Holy Bible)*

Jesus moved the world with His words. And we can do the same.

> *[21] Then said Jesus to them again, Peace be unto you: as my Father hath sent me, even so send I you. [22] And when he had said this, he breathed on them, and saith unto them, Receive ye the Holy Ghost: [23] Whose soever sins ye remit, they are remitted unto them; and whose soever sins ye retain, they are retained. (John 20:21-23)*

> *Remember the word that I said unto you, The servant is not greater than his lord. If they have persecuted me, they will also persecute you; if they have kept my sayings, they will keep yours also. (John 15:20)*

The faith of God resides inside of every believer. The amazing power, possibilities and responsibilities God has given to us, that we have in Christ, demonstrates the unbounded love God has for us. And it is more abundantly demonstrated in that notwithstanding all the demonstrations of love and power that Jesus did on earth, we are destined to do even greater works than Jesus did.

> *[12] Verily, verily, I say unto you, He that believeth on me, the works that I do shall he do also; and greater works than these shall he do; because I go unto my Father. [13] And whatsoever ye shall ask in my name, that will I do, that the Father may be glorified in the Son. [14] If ye shall ask any thing in my name, I will do it. (John 14:12-14)*

Jesus lives to intercede on our behalf. He is our apostle, gone forth to God on our behalf to confess before God what we confess in the earth.

Whosoever therefore shall confess me before men, him will I confess also before my Father which is in heaven. (Matthew 10:32)

Wherefore, holy brethren, partakers of the heavenly calling, consider the Apostle and High Priest of our profession, Christ Jesus; (Hebrews 3:1)

[24] But this man, because he continueth ever, hath an unchangeable priesthood.
[25] Wherefore he is able also to save them to the uttermost that come unto God by him, seeing he ever liveth to make intercession for them. (Hebrews 7:24-25)

[14] And this is the confidence that we have in him, that, if we ask any thing according to his will, he heareth us: [15] And if we know that he hear us, whatsoever we ask, we know that we have the petitions that we desired of him. (I John 5:14-15, NKJV)

[23] Let us hold fast the profession of our faith without wavering; {for he is faithful that promised;}. (Hebrews 10:23)

We've come full circle. We can only confess what is in our heart. If the Word of God is in our hearts in abundance, then the Word of God – the same words that Jesus spoke - is what we will speak. And abundant life, peace, wisdom, and success will manifest in our lives. Mary sat at the feet of Jesus to hear him, to fill her heart with his word. Jesus said Mary had chosen the one thing that was necessary.

> *[38] Now it came to pass, as they went, that he entered into a certain village: and a certain woman named Martha received him into her house. [39] And she had a sister called Mary, which also sat at Jesus's feed, and heard his word. [40] But Martha was cumbered about much serving, and came to him, and said, Lord, dost thou not care that my sister hath left me to serve alone? Bid her therefore that she help me. [41] And Jesus answered and said unto her, Martha, Martha, thou art careful and troubled about many things: [42] But one thing is needful: and Mary hath chosen that good part, which shall not be taken away from her. (Luke 10:38-42)*

Let the word of Christ dwell in you richly in all wisdom; teaching and admonishing one another in psalms and hymns and spiritual songs, singing with grace in your hearts to the Lord. And whatsoever ye do in word or deed, do all in the name of the Lord Jesus, giving thanks to God and the Father by him. (Colossians 3:16-17)

The word is nigh thee, even in thy mouth, and in thy heart: that is, the word of faith, which we preach. (Romans 10:8)

CHAPTER IX

INCREASE YOUR ABILITY TO RECEIVE FROM GOD

But Jesus said unto them, A prophet is not without honour, but in his own country, and among his own kin, and in his own house. And he could there do no mighty work, save that he laid his hands upon a few sick folk, and healed them. And he marveled because of their unbelief. (Mark 6:4-6)

We can be in the presence of God and even receive from God yet be so full of unbelief that it causes God to marvel. Imagine what can happen in our lives if we begin to believe!!

What we think of God, how we see God, even how we see ourselves, does not impact how much God loves us. But it does impact our ability to have the fulness of God's love manifested in our lives. Because of how the people in Jesus' hometown thought of him, they couldn't receive the love of God manifested through the "mighty works" of Jesus.

There are habits of behavior, habits of thought, and habits of belief, that we can learn, remember, develop, and intentionally undertake so that Jesus can do "mighty works" in our lives.

<u>God loves you</u>

God is not mad at you.

> *For God sent Christ Jesus to take the punishment for our sins and to end all God's anger against us. He used Christ's blood and our faith as the means of saving us from his wrath. . .. (Romans 3:25, TLB)*

> *[38] Be it known unto you therefore, men and brethren, that through this man is preached unto you the forgiveness of sins: [39] And by him all that believe are justified from all things, from which ye could not be justified by the law of Moses. (Acts 13:38-39)*

> *But to him that worketh not, but believeth on him that justifieth the ungodly, his faith is counted for righteousness. (Romans 4:5)*

> *Let us therefore come boldly unto the throne of grace, that we may obtain mercy, and find grace to help in time of need. (Hebrews 4:16)*

<u>God is waiting to answer your cry for help</u>

> *Call upon Me in the day of trouble; I will deliver you, and you shall glorify Me. (Psalm 50:15, NKJV)*

> *For the eyes of the Lord are over the righteous, and his ears are open unto their prayers . . . (I Peter 3:12, NKJV)*

[14] And this is the confidence that we have in him, that, if we ask anything according to his will, he heareth us: [15] And if we know that he hear us, whatsoever we ask, we know that we have the petitions that we desired of him. (I John 5:14-15)

[7] Ask, and it shall be given you; seek, and ye shall find; knock, and it shall be opened unto you: [8] For every one that asketh receiveth; and he that seeketh findeth; and to him that knocketh it shall be opened. [9] Or what man is there of you, whom if his son ask bread, will he give him a stone? [10] Or if he ask a fish, will he give him a serpent? [11] If ye then, being evil, know how to give good gifts unto your children, how much more shall your Father which is in heaven give good things to them that ask him? (Matthew 7:7-11)

Do all things in faith

But without faith it is impossible to please him: for he that cometh to God must believe that he is, and that he is a rewarder of them that diligently seek him. (Hebrews 11:6)

For therein is the righteousness of God revealed from faith to faith; as it is written, The just shall live by faith. (Romans 1:17)

Faith releases God's power in our lives.

[19] Then came the disciples to Jesus apart, and said, Why could not we cast him out?

> *[20] And Jesus said unto them, Because of your unbelief: for verily I say unto you, If ye have faith as a grain of mustard seed, ye shall say unto this mountain, Remove hence to yonder place; and it shall remove; and nothing shall be impossible unto you. (Matthew 17:19-20)*

> *[27] She had heard all about the wonderful miracles Jesus did . . . [28] . . . she thought to herself, "If I can just touch his clothing, I will be healed." [29] And sure enough, as soon as she had touched him, the bleeding stopped and she knew she was well!" . . . [34] And he said to her, "Daughter, your faith has made you well; go in peace, healed of your disease." (Mark 5:27-35, TLB)*

Grow in faith

Our ability to receive from God is predicated on our level of faith in God. Although every man has been given a measure of faith, we can grow in faith.

Peter walked on water with little faith.

> *[29] And he said, Come. And when Peter was come down out of the ship, he walked on the water, to go to Jesus. [30] But when he saw the wind boisterous, he was afraid: and beginning to sink, he cried, saying, Lord, save me. [31] And immediately Jesus stretched forth his hand, and caught him, and said unto him, o thou of little faith, wherefore didst thou doubt? (Matthew 14:29-31)*

The centurion, who believed his servant would be healed if Jesus only spoke the word, had great faith.

> *[8] The centurion answered and said, Lord, I am not worthy that thou shouldest come under my roof: but speak the word only, and my servant shall be healed. . . . [10] When Jesus heard it, he marveled, and said to them that followed, Verily I say unto you, I have not found so great faith, no, not in Israel. . . . [13] And Jesus said unto the centurion, Go thy way; and as thou hast believed, so be it done unto thee. And his servant was healed in the selfsame hour. (Matthew 8:8-13)*

We can grow in faith.

> *We are bound to thank God always for you, brethren, as it is meet, because that your faith groweth exceedingly, and the charity of every one of you all toward each other aboundeth. (II Thessalonians 1:3)*

We grow in faith by hearing the Word of God.

> *So then faith cometh by hearing, and hearing by the Word of God. (Romans 10:17)*

Have a "now" faith, not a "someday" faith

God is not bound by time.

> *Behold, the days come, saith the Lord, that the plowman shall overtake the reaper, and the*

> *treader of grapes him that soweth seed; and the mountains shall drop sweet wine, and all the hills shalt melt. (Amos 9:13)*

> *[24] Martha saith unto him, I know that he shall rise again in the resurrection at the last day. [25] Jesus said unto her, I am the resurrection, and the life . . .*
> *(John 11:24-25)*

God is not bounded by earthly conditions.

> *[34] Then said Mary unto the angel, How shall this be, seeing I know not a man? [35] And the angel answered and said unto her, The Holy Ghost shall come upon thee, and the power of the Highest shall overshadow thee: therefore also that holy thing which shall be born of thee shall be called the Son of God. . . . [37] For with God nothing shall be impossible. (Luke 1:34-37)*

It is never too late for God.

> *[1] From inside the fish Jonah prayed to the Lord his God. . .. [10] And the Lord commanded the fish, and it vomited Jonah onto dry land. (Jonah 2:1-10, NIV)*

> *[5] There was in the days of Herod, the king of Judaea, a certain priest named Zacharias, of the course of Abia; and his wife was of the daughters of Aaron, and her name was Elisabeth. [6] And they were both righteous before God, walking in all the commandments and ordinances of the Lord blameless. [7] And*

> *they had no child, because that Elisabeth was barren, and they both were now well stricken in years. (Luke 1:5-7)*
>
> *[11] And there appeared unto him an angel of the Lord standing on the right side of the altar of incense, [12] And when Zacharias saw him, he was troubled, and fear fell upon him*
> *[13] But the angel said unto him, Fear not, Zacharias; for thy prayer is heard; and thy wife Elisabeth shall bear thee a son, and thou shalt call his name John. (Luke 1:11-13)*
>
> *Now Elisabeth's full time came that she should be delivered; and she brought forth a son. (Luke 1:57)*

But sometimes we have so much comfort in our discomfort that we'd rather remain in, or turn back to, what we don't want, rather than use our faith to move toward God's promises that we do want.

> *Didn't we say to you in Egypt, 'Leave us alone; let us serve the Egyptians'? It would have been better for us to serve the Egyptians than to die in the desert!"*
> *(Exodus 14:12, NIV)*
>
> *And the Lord said to Moses, "Why do you cry to Me? Tell the children of Israel to go forward. (Exodus 14:15)*

Sometimes we travel the long way to God's promises because we have too little faith to receive the promise right away.

> *[17] When Pharaoh let the people go, God did not lead them on the road through the Philistine country, though that was shorter. For God said, "If they face war, they might change their minds and return to Egypt." [18] So God led the people around by the desert road toward the Red Sea. . .. (Exodus 13:17-18, NIV)*

Sometimes we are more focused on the problem than the promise.

> *[37] And some of them said, Could not this man, which opened the eyes of the blind have caused that even this man should not have died? [38] Jesus therefore again groaning in himself cometh to the grave. It was a cave, and a stone lay upon it. [39] Jesus said, Take ye away the stone. Martha, the sister of him that was dead, saith unto him, Lord, by this time he stinketh: for he hath been dead four days. (John 11:37-39)*

Sometimes we are more focused on the process than the promise.

> *[5] And a certain man was there, which had an infirmity thirty and eight years. [6] When Jesus saw him lie, and knew that he had been now a long time in that case, he saith unto him, Wilt thou be made whole? [7] The impotent man answered him, Sir, I have no man, when the water is troubled, to put me into the pool: but while I am coming another steppeth down before me. (John 5:5-7)*

And sometimes we forget that God sent his love to give to us, not to take from us.

> *[39] And she had a sister called Mary, which also sat at Jesus' feet and heard his word. [40] But Martha was cumbered about much serving, and came to him, and said, Lord, dost thou not care that my sister hath left me to serve alone? Bid her therefore that she help me. [41] And Jesus answered and said unto her, Martha, Martha, thou art careful and troubled about many things: [42) But one thing is needful: and Mary hath chosen that good part, which shall not be taken away from her. (Luke 10:39-42)*

> *[28] Then said they unto him, What shall we do, that we might work the works of God? [29] Jesus answered and said unto them, This is the work of God, that ye believe on him whom he hath sent. (John 6:28-29)*

> *Herein is love, not that we loved God, but that he loved us, and sent his Son to be the propitiation for our sins. (I John 4:10)*

Expect the favor of God. God is faithful. God cannot lie. God is love. And His words are eternal. Whatever God has said he must fulfill. Even when we are in the midst of the most expansive blessing we've ever seen – from the outhouse to the penthouse – we haven't gotten all God has for us. Even after we've plundered the enemy. Even after God has washed away everyone that wished us ill. Even when the angels have gone before us and removed every hindrance, every illness, and everyone that has an evil report. Even then, God is not done. Don't stop to make peace with a land you should be either capturing, simply passing through, or that is in any event less than God's best for you. Keep releasing faith to move forward.

> *[27] I will send my fear before thee, and will destroy all the people to whom thou shalt come, and I will make all thine enemies turn their backs unto thee. . .. [29] I will not drive them out from before thee in one year; lest the land become desolate, and the beast of the field multiply against thee. [30] By little and little I will drive them out from before thee, until thou be increased, and inherit the land. [31] And I will set thy bounds from the Red sea even unto the sea of the Philistines, and from the desert unto the river: for I will deliver the inhabitants of the land into your hand; and thou shall drive them out before thee. [32] Thou shalt make no covenant with them, nor with their gods. (Exodus 23:27-32)*

Ask for and expect more than you can possibly do <u>on your own</u>

> *[13] And whatsoever ye shall ask in my name, that will I do, that the Father may be glorified in the Son. [14] If ye shall ask any thing in my name, I will do it. (John 14:13-14)*

> *[21] Then Martha said unto Jesus, Lord, if thou hadst been here, my brother had not died. [22] But I know, that even now, whatsoever thou wilt ask of God, God will give it thee. (John 11:21-22)*

> *[28] And Peter answered him and said, Lord, if it be thou, bid me come unto thee on the water. [29] And he said, Come. And when*

Peter was come down out of the ship, he walked on the water, to go to Jesus. (Matthew 14:28-29)

[28] And when he was come into the house, the blind men came to him: and Jesus saith unto them, Believe ye that I am able to do this? They said unto him, Yea, Lord.
[29] Then touched he their eyes, saying, According to your faith be it unto you.
[30] And their eyes were opened; . . .
(Matthew 9:28-30)

Seek God's plan and God's wisdom in every endeavor

[11] "For I know the plans I have for you," declares the Lord, "plans to prosper you and not to harm you, plans to give you hope and a future. [12] Then you will call upon me and come and pray to me, and I will listen to you. (Jeremiah 29:11-12, NIV)

[2] This is what the Lord says, he who made the earth, the Lord who formed it and established it – the Lord is his name: [3] 'Call to me and I will answer you and tell you great and unsearchable things you do not know.' (Jeremiah 33:2-3, NIV)

If any of you lack wisdom, let him ask of God, that giveth to all men liberally, and upbraideth not; and it shall be given him. (James 1:5)

Any plan outside of God's plan is a waste of time, no matter how hard you work on it.

John answered and said, A man can receive nothing, except it be given him from heaven. (John 3:27)

[1] Unless the Lord builds the house, they labor in vain who build it; unless the Lord guards the city, the watchman stays awake in vain. [2] It is vain for you to rise up early, to sit up late, to eat the bread of sorrows; for so He gives His beloved sleep. (Psalm 127:1-2, NKJV)

<u>Do everything God has told you to do</u>

When you have heard from God, do everything God has told you to do. The widow of the prophet went further into debt at the word of Elisha in order to get out of debt. The level of her obedience determined the level of her prosperity.

[1] Now there cried a certain woman of the wives of the sons of the prophets unto Elisha, saying, Thy servant my husband is dead; and thou knowest that thy servant did fear the Lord: and the creditor is coming to take unto him my two sons to be bondmen. [2] And Elisha said unto her, What shall I do for thee? Tell me, what hast thou in the house? And she said, Thine handmaid hath not any thing in the house, save a pot of oil. [3] Then he said, Go, borrow thee vessels abroad of all thy neighbours, even empty vessels; borrow not a few. [4] And when thou are come in, thou shalt shut the door upon thee and upon thy sons, and shalt pour out into all those vessels, and thou shalt set aside that which is full. [5] So she went from him, and shut the door upon her and upon her sons, who brought the

> *vessels to her; and she poured out. [6] And it came to pass, when the vessels were full, that she said unto her son, Bring me yet a vessel. And he said unto her, There is not a vessel more. And the oil stayed. [7] Then she came and told the man of God. And he said, Go, sell the oil, and pay thy debt, and live thou and thy children of the rest. (2 Kings 4:1-7)*

Doing whatever you know God has called you to do, includes doing all the little things that you know God has called you to do.

> *[9] So Naaman came with his horses and with his chariot, and stood at the door of the house of Elisha. [10] And Elisha sent a messenger unto him, saying, Go and wash in Jordan seven times, and thy flesh shall come again to thee, and thou shalt be clean. [11] But Naaman was wroth, and went away, and said, Behold, I thought, He will surely come out to me, and stand, and call on the name of the Lord his God, and strike his hand over the place, and recover the leper. [12] Are not Abana and Pharpar, rivers of Damacus, better than all the waters of Israel? May I not wash in them, and be clean? So he turned and went away in a rage. [13] And his servants came near, and spake unto him, and said, My father, if the prophet had bid thee do some great thing, wouldest thou not have done it? How much rather then, when he saith to thee, Wash, and be clean? [14] Then went he down, and dipped himself seven times in Jordan,*

> *according to the saying of the man of God: and his flesh came again like unto the flesh of a little child, and he was clean. (2 Kings 5:9-14)*

The first Biblically recorded miracle of Jesus *resulted from* the little thing of pouring water into a pot. And that little thing *resulted in* the disciples believing in Jesus.

> *[3] And when they wanted wine, the mother of Jesus saith unto him, They have no wine. . . .*
> *[5] His mother saith unto the servants, Whatsoever he saith unto you, do it. . . .*
> *[7] Jesus saith unto them, Fill the waterpots with water, And they filled them up to the brim. (John 2:3-7)*

> *[9] When the ruler of the feast had tasted the water that was made wine, and knew not whence it was: (but the servants which drew the water knew) the governor of the feast called the bridegroom, [10] And saith unto him, Every man at the beginning doth set forth good wine; and when men have well drunk, then that which is worse: but thou hast kept the good wine until now. (John 2:9-10)*

> *This beginning of miracles did Jesus in Cana of Galilee, and manifested forth his glory; and his disciples believed on him. (John 2:11)*

Always affirm the Word of God (in behavior and speech

That is what Moses did when God said don't go.

> *[42] But the Lord said to me, "Tell them, 'Do not go up and fight, because I will not be with*

> *you. You will be defeated by your enemies.'" [43] So I told you, but you would not listen. You rebelled against the Lord's command and in your arrogance you marched up into the hill country. [44] The Amorites who lived in those hills came out against you; they chased you like a swarm of bees and beat you down from Seir all the way to Hormah. [45] You came back and wept before the Lord, but he paid no attention to your weeping and turned a deaf ear to you.*
> *(Deuteronomy 1:42-45, NIV)*

It is what Joshua and Caleb did when God said go.

> *[6] And Joshua the son of Nun, and Caleb the son of Jephunneh, which were of them that searched the land, rent their clothes: [7] And they spake unto all the company of the children of Israel, saying, The land, which we passed through to search it, is an exceeding good land. [8] If the Lord delight in us, then he will bring us into this land, and give it us; a land which floweth with milk and honey.*
> *[8] Only rebel not ye against the Lord, neither fear ye the people of the land; for they are bread for us: their defence is departed from them, and the Lord is with us: fear them not.*
> *(Numbers 14:6-9)*

And it is a part of what Peter learned on the housetop.

> *[13] And there came a voice to him, Rise, Peter; kill, and eat. [14] But Peter said, Not so, Lord; for I have never eaten any thing that is common or unclean. [15] And the voice spake unto him again the second time, What*

God hath cleansed, that call not thou common. (Acts 10:13-15)

Don't delay when God says move

And Joshua said unto the children of Israel, How long are ye slack to go to possess the land, which the Lord God of your fathers hath given you? (Joshua 18:3)

Whatever God tells you to conquer you have the strength to conquer

[10] Then Moses said to the Lord, "O my Lord, I am not eloquent, neither before nor since You have spoken to Your servant; but I am slow of speech and slow of tongue."
[11] So the Lord said to him, "Who has made man's mouth? Or who makes the mute, the deaf, the seeing, or the blind? Have not I, the Lord? [12] Now therefore, go, and I will be with your mouth and teach you what you shall say." (Exodus 4:10-12, NKJV)

[14] The Lord turned to him and said, "Go in the strength you have and save Israel out of Midian's hand. Am I not sending you?"
[15] "But Lord," Gideon asked, "how can I save Israel? My clan is the weakest in Manasseh, and I am the least in my family."
[16] The Lord answered, "I will be with you, and you will strike down all the Midianites together." (Judges 6:14-16, NIV)

[13] Moses answered the people, "Do not be afraid. Stand firm and you will see the deliverance the Lord will bring you today. The

> *Egyptians you see today you will never see again. [14] The Lord will fight for you; you need only to be still." [15] Then the Lord said to Moses, "Why are you crying out to me? Tell the Israelites to move on. [16] Raise your staff and stretch out your hand over the sea to divide the water so that the Israelites can go through the sea on dry ground.*
> *(Exodus 14:13-16, NIV)*

> *[26] And when the disciples saw him walking on the sea, they were troubled, saying, It is a spirit; and they cried out for fear. [27] But straightway Jesus spake unto them, saying, Be of good cheer; it is I; be not afraid. [28] And Peter answered him and said, Lord, if it be thou, bid me to come unto thee on the water. [29] And he said, Come. And when Peter was come down out of the ship, he walked on the water, to go to Jesus.*
> *(Matthew 14:26-29 JKV)*

Do not mourn after a door that God has closed, a relationship that God has ended, or an idol that God has removed from your life.

> *Now the Lord said to Samuel, "How long will you mourn for Saul, seeing I have rejected him from reigning over Israel? Fill your horn with oil, and go; I am sending you to Jesse the Bethlehemite. For I have provided Myself a king among his sons." (I Samuel 16:1)*

Do not declare fear where God has declared victory. It will delay your destiny.

[25] And they returned from spying out the land after forty days. ... [27] Then they told him, and said: "We went to the land where you sent us. It truly flows with milk and honey, and this is its fruit. Nevertheless the people who dwell in the land are strong; the cities are fortified and very large; . . . [33] And they gave the children of Israel a bad report of the land which they had spied out, saying, "The land through which we have gone as spies is a land that devours its inhabitants, and all the people whom we saw in it are men of great stature. . . . and we were like grasshoppers in our own sight, and so we were in their sight." (Numbers 13:25-33)

Then the Lord said to Moses: "How long will these people reject Me? And how long will they not believe Me, with all the signs which I have performed among them? (Numbers 14:11, NKJV)

[22] {B}ecause all those men which have seen my glory, and my miracles which I did in Egypt and in the wilderness, and have tempted me now these ten times, and have not hearkened to my voice; [23] Surely they shall not see the land which I sware unto their fathers, neither shall any of them that provoked me see it. [24] But my servant Caleb, because he had another spirit with him, and hath followed me fully, him will I bring into the land whereinto he went; and his seed shall possess it. (Numbers 14:22-24)

[34] After the number of days in which ye searched the land, even forty days, each day

for a year, shall ye bear your iniquities, even forty years, and ye shall know my breach of promise. (Numbers 14:34)

Put your trust in God, not in man

But you have planted wickedness, you have reaped evil, you have eaten the fruit of deception. Because you have depended on your own strength and on your many warriors, . . . (Hosea 10:13, NIV)

[7] Blessed is the man that trusteth in the Lord, and whose hope the Lord is. [8] For he shall be as a tree planted by the waters, and that spreadeth out her roots by the river, and shall not see when heat cometh, but her leaf shall be green: and shall not be careful in the year of drought, neither shall cease from yielding fruit. (Jeremiah 17:7-8)

Surely God is my help; the Lord is the one who sustains me. (Psalm 54:4, NIV)

[14] And this is the confidence that we have in him, that, if we ask any thing according to his will, he heareth us: [15] And if we know that he hear us, whatsoever we ask, we know that we have the petitions that we desired of him. (I John 5:14-15)

Remember that God is your source

[23] This is what the Lord says: "Let not the wise man boast of his wisdom or the strong man boast of his strength or the rich man boast of his riches, [24] but let him who

> *boasts boast about this: that he understands and knows me, that I am the Lord, who exercises kindness, justice and righteousness on earth, for in these I delight," declares the Lord. (Jeremiah 9:23-24, NIV)*

> *And you shall remember the Lord your God, for it is He who gives you power to get wealth, that He may establish His covenant which He swore to your fathers, as it is this day. (Deuteronomy 8:18, NKJV)*

> *[6] For promotion cometh neither from the east, nor from the west, nor from the south. [7] But God is the judge: he putteth down one, and setteth up another. (Psalms 75:6-7)*

As children of God, whenever we are in reliance on anything or anyone but God, we are not in our right mind. As in the parable of the prodigal son, when the younger son came to himself he returned to his father's house.

> *And when he came to himself, he said, How many hired servants of my father's have bread enough to spare, and I perish with hunger! (Luke 15:17)*

> *Humble yourselves therefore under the mighty hand of God, that he may exalt you in due time. (I Peter 5:6)*

The battle is always spiritual

> *While we look not at the things which are seen, but at the things which are not seen: for the things which are seen are temporal; but*

the things which are not seen are eternal. (II Corinthians 4:18)

[10] So Joshua did as Moses said to him, and fought with Amalek. And Moses, Aaron, and Hur went up to the top of the hill. [11] And so it was, when Moses held up his hand, that Israel prevailed; and when he let down his hand, Amalek prevailed. [12] But Moses' hands became heavy; so they took a stone and put it under him, and he sat on it. And Aaron and Hur supported his hands, one on one side, and the other on the other side; and his hands were steady until the going down of the sun. [13] So Joshua defeated Amalek and his people with the edge of the sword. (Exodus 17:10-13, NKJV)

[45] David said to the Philistine, "You come against me with sword and spear and javelin, but I come against you in the name of the Lord Almighty, the God of the armies of Israel, whom you have defied. [46] This day the Lord will hand you over to me, and I'll strike you down and cut off your head. Today I will give the carcasses of the Philistine army to the birds of the air and the beasts of the earth, and the whole world will know that there is a God in Israel. [47] All those gathered here will know that it is not by sword or spear that the Lord saves; for the battle is the Lord's and he will give all of you into our hands." (I Samuel 17:45-47, NIV)

For we wrestle not against flesh and blood, but against principalities, against powers, against the rules of the darkness of this world, against spiritual wickedness in high places. (Ephesians 6:12)

No matter what you see or hear in the physical realm, continually seek the Lord.

But the Lord said unto Samuel, Look not on his countenance, or on the height of his stature; because I have refused him: for the Lord seeth not as man seeth: for man looketh on the outward appearance, but the Lord looketh on the heart. (I Samuel 16:7)

[15] And when the servant of the man of God arose early and went out, there was an army, surrounding the city with horses and chariots. And his servant said to him, "alas, my master! What shall we do?" [16] So he answered, "Do not fear, for those who are with us are more than those who are with them."
[17] And Elisha prayed, and said, "Lord, I pray, open his eyes that he may see." Then the Lord opened the eyes of the young man, and he saw. And behold, the mountain was full or horses and chariots of fire all around Elisha. (2 Kings 6:15-17, NKJV)

For we walk by faith, not by sight. (II Corinthians 5:7)

Keep your eyes on God

Peter walked on water until he took his eyes off Jesus. Peter moved from faith to fear when he took his eyes off Jesus. Don't judge the Word of God. Receive the Word of God and walk in the Word of God that you have received. Then you will walk in power, boldness and supernatural ability. Based on one word from Jesus, Peter walked on the storm-tossed sea until he began to judge what he was doing given the circumstances.

> *[26] And when the disciples saw him walking on the sea, they were troubled, saying, It is a spirit; and they cried out for fear. [27] But straightway Jesus spake unto them, saying, Be of good cheer; it is I; be not afraid. [28] And Peter answered him and said, Lord, if it be thou, bid me to come unto thee on the water. [29] And he said, Come. And when Peter was come down out of the ship, he walked on the water, to go to Jesus. (Matthew 14:26-29)*

> *But when he saw the wind boisterous, he was afraid; and beginning to sink, he cried, saying, Lord, save me. (Matthew 14:30)*

Peter was a professional fisherman. He knew before he got out of the boat - before he looked at the boisterous wind, and before he became afraid - that he couldn't walk on water in his own ability. That was not a revelation that he received from God just as he began to sink. The before and after difference is that when Peter stepped out of the boat, his focus was solely on Jesus and the word that Jesus gave him, "Come." When Peter was focused on Jesus, and moved on the word he got from Jesus, Peter walked in the ability of Jesus. When Peter was focused on Peter and the storm, Peter walked in the ability of Peter and began to sink. When we move in faith on the Word of God, we walk in the supernatural power of the Word of God.

> *Jesus looked at them intently, then said, "Without God, it is utterly impossible. But with God everything is possible." (Mark 10:27, TLB)*

Note that this scripture doesn't say all things are possible "by" God. It all things are possible "with" God. Everything is possible in our lives when we move with God!!

<u>Jesus already paid for it ALL</u>

Jesus died once for all people and all things for all times. Don't justify the absence of anything that has already been paid for with the blood of Jesus. The blood of Jesus completely paid for every good thing.

> *[4] Jesus answered and said unto them, Go and show John again those things which ye do hear and see: [5] The blind receive their sight, and the lame walk, the lepers are cleansed, and the deaf hear, the dead are raised up, and the poor have the gospel preached to them. (Matthew 11:4-5)*

> *The thief comes only in order to steal and kill and destroy. I came that they may have and enjoy life, and have it in abundance (to the full, till it overflows) (John 10:10, AMP)*

> *Every good gift and every perfect gift is from above, and cometh down from the Father of lights, with whom is no variableness, neither shadow of turning (James 1:17)*

Receive all that Jesus died for you to receive. While Martha was trying to serve Him, Jesus lauded Mary for receiving from Him. Similarly, Jesus told Peter not that Peter should serve Him, but that He must serve him.

> *And he is not served by human hands, as if he needed anything, because he himself gives all*

> *men life and breath and everything else. (Acts 17:25, NIV)*

> *Peter saith unto him, Thou shalt never wash my feet. Jesus answered him, If I wash thee not, thou hast no part of me. (John 13:8)*

> *For even the Son of Man did not come to be served, but to serve, and to give His life a ransom for many. (Mark 10:45, NKJV)*

> *[27] And whosoever will be chief among you, let him be your servant: [28] Even as the Son of man came not to be ministered unto, but to minister, and to give his life a ransom for many. (Matthew 20:27-28)*

Don't limit your ability to receive from God by professing some false sense of humility or piety based on the idea that poverty in any area of your life evidences holiness or a lesson from God. True humility and piety accept the righteousness of God through Christ and accepts all that Jesus died for us to receive.

> *For as many as are the promises of God, they all find their Yes {answer} in Him {Christ}. . . (II Corinthians 1:20, AMP)*

> *Now we have received, not the spirt of the world, but the spirit which is of God; that we might know the things that are freely given to us of God. (I Corinthians 2:12)*

> *For I will be leaning toward you with favor and regard for you, rendering you fruitful, multiplying you, and establishing you and*

> *ratifying my covenant with you.*
> *(Leviticus 26:9, AMP)*

> *[8] And God is able to make all grace abound toward you; that ye, always having all sufficiency in all things, may abound to every good work: . . . [11] Being enriched in every thing to all bountifulness, which causeth through us thanksgiving to God.*
> *(II Corinthians 9:8-11)*

> *[28] Then Peter began to say unto him, Lo, we have left all, and have followed thee.*
> *[29] And Jesus answered and said, Verily I say unto you, There is no man that hath left house, or brethren, or sisters, or father, or mother, or wife, or children, or lands, for my sake, and the gospel's. [30] But he shall receive an hundredfold now in this time, houses, and brethren, and sisters, and mothers, and children, and lands, with persecutions; and in the world to come eternal life. (Mark 10:28-30)*

When we know who God is, we will ask of him and he will provide.

> *Jesus answered and said unto her, If thou knewest the gift of God, and who it is that saith to thee, Give me to drink; thou wouldest have asked of him, and he would have given thee living water. (John 4:10)*

> *Ask of Me, and I will give You the nations as Your inheritance, and the uttermost parts of the earth as Your possession.*
> *(Psalm 2:8, AMP)*

If ye abide in me, and my words abide in you, ye shall ask what ye will, and it shall be done unto you. (John 15:7)

The problem is never in having riches. God is the source of our abundance and takes pleasure in our prosperity.

Blessed be the Lord, Who daily loads us with benefits, The God of our salvation! Selah. (Psalm 68:19, NKJV)

Let them shout for joy, and be glad, that favour my righteous cause: yea, let them say continually, Let the Lord be magnified, which hath pleasure in the prosperity of his servant. (Psalms 35:27)

For ye know the grace of our Lord Jesus Christ, that, though he was rich, yet for your sakes he became poor, that ye through his poverty might be rich. (II Corinthians 8:9)

Beloved, I wish above all things that thou mayest prosper and be in health, even as thy soul prospereth. (3 John 2)

The problem is trusting in riches.

[23] And Jesus looked round about, and saith unto his disciples, How hardly shall they that have riches enter into the kingdom of God! [24] And the disciples were astonished at his words. But Jesus answereth again, and saith unto them, Children, how hard is it for them that trust in riches to enter into the kingdom of God! (Mark 10:23-24)

As children of God, we are accepted by God.[97] And we can trust and walk in the wisdom, peace and favor of God.

> *Peace I leave with you, my peace I give unto you: not as the world giveth, give I unto you. Let not your heart be troubled, neither let it be afraid. (John 14:27)*
>
> *Fools mock at sin, but among the upright there is the favor of God. (Proverbs 14:9, NKJV)*
>
> *[19] Then was the secret revealed unto Daniel in a night vision. Then Daniel blessed the God of heaven. [20] Daniel answered and said, Blessed be the name of God for ever and ever: for wisdom and might are his: [21] And he changeth the times and the seasons: he removeth kings, and setteth up kings: he giveth wisdom unto the wise, and knowledge to them that know understanding: [22] he revealeth the deep and secret things: he knoweth what is in the darkness, and the light dwelleth with him. [23] I thank thee, and praise thee, O thou God of my fathers, who hast given me wisdom and might, and hast made known unto me now what we desired of thee: . . . (Daniel 2:19-23)*
>
> *If any of you lack wisdom, let him ask of God, that giveth to all men liberally, and*

[97] *The word "accepted" was translated from the Greek word "charitoo" which means "highly favored."*

> *upbraideth not; and it shall be given him. (James 1:5)*

People turn to God when they see Christians walking in the wisdom, power, peace and favor of God.

> *[25] Then king Darius wrote unto all people, nations, and languages, that dwell in all the earth; Peace be multiplied unto you. [26] I make a decree, That in every dominion of my kingdom men tremble and fear before the God of Daniel: for he is the living God, and stedfast for ever, and his kingdom that which shall not be destroyed, and his dominion shall be even unto the end. [27] He delivereth and rescueth, and he worketh signs and wonders in heaven and in earth, who hath delivered Daniel from the power of the lions. (Daniel 6:25-27)*

> *[1] Then Jesus six days before the Passover came to Bethany, where Lazarus was which had been dead, whom he raised from the dead. [2] There they made him a supper; and Martha served: but Lazarus was one of them that sat at the table with him. . .. [9] Much people of the Jews therefore knew that he was there: and they came not for Jesus' sake only but that they might see Lazarus also, whom he had raised from the dead. [10] But the chief priests consulted that they might put Lazarus also to death; [11] Because that by reason of him many of the Jews went away, and believed on Jesus. (John 12:1-11)*

> *[25] And at midnight Paul and Silas prayed, and sang praises unto God: and the prisoners*

> *heard them. [26] And suddenly there was a great earthquake, so that the foundations of the prison were shaken: and immediately all the doors were opened, and every one's bands were loosed. [27] And the keeper of the prison awaking out of his sleep, and seeing the prison doors open, he drew out his sword, and would have killed himself, supposing that the prisoners had been fled. [28] But Paul cried with a loud voice, saying, Do thyself no harm: for we are all here. [29] Then he called for a light and sprang in, and came trembling, and fell down before Paul and Silas, [30] And brought them out, and said, Sirs, what must I do to be saved? (Acts 16:25-30)*

> *[32] And it came to pass, as Peter passed throughout all quarters, he came down also to the saints which dwelt at Lydda. [33] And there he found a certain man named Aeneas, which had kept his bed eight years, and was sick of the palsy. [34] And Peter said unto him, Aeneas, Jesus Christ maketh thee whole: arise, and make thy bed. And he arose immediately. [35] And all that dwelt at Lydda and Saron saw him, and turned to the Lord. (Acts 9:32-35)*

God is glorified when our life is fruitful.

> *[14] And beholding the man which was healed standing with them, they could say nothing against it. [15] But when they had commanded them to go aside out of the council, they conferred among themselves, [16] Saying, What shall we do to these men? For that indeed a notable miracle hath been*

> *done by them is manifest to all them that dwell in Jerusalem; and we cannot deny it. . . . [21] So when they had further threatened them, they let them go, finding nothing how they might punish them because of the people: for all men glorified God for that which was done. (Acts 4:14-21)*

> *[7] If ye abide in me, and my words abide in you, ye shall ask what ye will, and it shall be done unto you. [8] Herein is my Father glorified that ye bear much fruit; so shall ye be my disciples. (John 15:7-8)*

All of God's grace is available to all of God's children.

> *[8] So when even was come, the lord of the vineyard saith unto his steward, Call the labourers, and give them their hire, beginning from the last unto the first. [9] And when they came that were hired about the eleventh hour, they received every man a penny. [10] But when the first came, they supposed that they should have received more; and they likewise received every man a penny. [11] And when they had received it, they murmured against the goodman of the house, [12] Saying, These last have wrought but one hour, and thou hast made them equal unto us, which have borne the burden and heat of the day. [13] But he answered one of them, and said, Friend, I do thee no wrong; didst not thou agree with me for a penny? [14] Take that thine is, and go thy way: I will give unto this last, even as unto thee. [15] Is it not lawful for me to do what I will with mine own? Is thine eye evil, because*

*I am good? [16] So the last shall be first, and
the first last: for many be called, but few
chosen. (Matthew 20:8-16)*

*[39] And one of the malefactors which were
hanged railed on him, saying, If thou be
Christ, save thyself and us. [40] But the other
answering rebuked him, saying, Dost not thou
fear God, seeing thou art in the same
condemnation? [41] And we indeed justly; for
we receive the due reward of our deeds: but
this man hath done nothing amiss. [42] And
he said unto Jesus, Lord, remember me when
thou comest into thy kingdom. [43] And Jesus
said unto him, Verily I say unto thee, To day
shalt thou be with me in paradise.
(Luke 23:39-43)*

Praise God throughout the journey

*[16] Rejoice evermore. [17] Pray without
ceasing. [18] In every thing give thanks: for
this is the will of God in Christ Jesus
concerning you. (I Thessalonians 5:16-18)*

By him, therefore let us offer the sacrifice of praise to God continually, that is, the fruit of our lips giving thanks to his name. (Hebrews 13:15)

Don't rejoice in the works of your hands

And they made a calf in those days, and offered sacrifice unto the idol, and rejoiced in the works of their own hands. (Acts 7:41)

> *[9] "I have seen these people," the Lord said to Moses, "and they are a stiff-necked people. [10] Now leave me alone so that my anger may burn against them and that I may destroy them, Then I will make you into a great nation." [11] But Moses sought the favor of the Lord his God. . . . [14] Then the Lord relented and did not bring on his people the disaster he had threatened.*
> *(Exodus 32:9-14, NIV)*

> *For who maketh thee to differ from another? And what hast thou that thou didst not receive? Now if thou didst receive it, why dost thou glory, as if thou hadst not received it?*
> *(I Corinthians 4:7)*

Remember the Lord thy God

After you enter the promised land; after God has cancelled the debt; prospered you; cured the sickness; healed the relationship; purchased the home; got you the job; did the impossible and the world is cheering *your* accomplishment . . . don't forget it was God that got you there.

> *[21] And upon a set day Herod, arrayed in royal apparel, sat upon his throne, and made an oration unto them. [22] And the people gave a shout, saying, It is the voice of a god, and not of a man. [23] And immediately the angel of the Lord smote him, because he gave not God the glory: and he was eaten of worms, and gave up the ghost. (Acts 12:21-23)*

> *[12] Then beware lest thou forget the Lord, which brought thee forth out of the land of Egypt, from the house of bondage. [13] Thou*

shalt fear the Lord thy God, and serve him, and shalt swear by his name. [14] Ye shall not go after other gods, of the gods of the people which are round about you. [15] {for the Lord thy God is a jealous God among you} lest the anger of the Lord thy God be kindled against thee, and destroy thee from off the face of the earth. (Deuteronomy 6:12-15)

But cleave unto the Lord your God, as ye have done unto this day. (Joshua 23:8)

As you walk in God's promises, continue to praise God.

When thou hast eaten and art full, then thou shalt bless the Lord thy God for the good land which he hath given thee. (Deuteronomy 8:10)

He who sacrifices thank offerings honors me, and he prepares the way so that I may show him the salvation of God. (Psalm 50:23, NIV)

. . . Those who honor me I will honor, but they that despise me shall be lightly esteemed. (I Samuel 2:30)

[1] And David spake unto the Lord the words of this song in the day that the Lord had delivered him out of the hand of all his enemies, and out of the hand of Saul: [2] And he said, the Lord is my rock, and my fortress, and my deliverer; [3] The God of my rock; in him will I trust: he is my shield, and the horn of my salvation, my high tower, and my refuge, my savior; thou savest me from violence. [4] I will call on the Lord, who is

> *worthy to be praised: so shall I be saved from mine enemies. (2 Samuel 22:1-4)*

> *[47] The Lord liveth; and blessed be my rock; and exalted be the God of the rock of my salvation. [48] It is God that avengeth me, and that bringeth down the people under me. [49] And that bringeth me forth from mine enemies: thou also hast lifted me up on high above them that rose up against me: thou hast delivered me from the violent man.*
> *[50] Therefore I will give thanks unto thee, O Lord, among the heathen, and I will sing praises unto thy name. (2 Samuel 22:47-50)*

God lives in the praises of his people.

> *But thou art holy, O thou that inhabitest the praises of Israel. (Psalms 22:3)*

<u>Be generous with whatever God has given you</u>

> *[9] And let us not be weary in well doing: for in due season we shall reap, if we faint not. [10] As we have therefore opportunity, let us do good unto all men, especially unto them who are of the household of faith. (Galatians 6:9-10)*

> *I have shewed you all things, how that so laboring ye ought to support the weak, and to remember the words of the Lord Jesus, how he said, It is more blessed to give than to receive. (Acts 20:35)*

> *God has given each of you some special abilities; be sure to use them to help each*

other, passing on to others God's many kinds of blessings. (I Peter 4:10, TLB)

So, two good things happen as a result of your gifts – those in need are helped, and they overflow with thanks to God.
(II Corinthians 9:12, TLB)

Don't forget to do good and to share what you have with those in need, for such sacrifices are very pleasing to him.
(Hebrews 13:16, TLB)

"Give, and it will be given to you: good measure, pressed down, shaken together, and running over will be put into your bosom. For with the same measure that you use, it will be measured back to you." (Luke 6:38, NIV)

Remember that God is never far, his mercies are forever new, and his love is everlasting

[38] For I am persuaded, that neither death, nor life, nor angels, nor principalities, nor powers, nor things present, nor things to come, [39] Nor height, nor depth, nor any other creature, shall be able to separate us from the love of God, which is in Christ Jesus our Lord. (Romans 8:38-39)

[22] It is of the Lord's mercies that we are not consumed, because his compassions fail not. [23] They are new every morning: great is thy faithfulness. [24] The Lord is my portion, saith my soul; therefore will I hope in him. [25] The Lord is good unto them that wait for

him, to the soul that seeketh him. (Lamentations 3:22-24)

[11] For I know the thoughts that I think toward you, saith the Lord, thoughts of peace, and not of evil, to give you an expected end. [12] Then shall ye call upon me, and ye shall go and pray unto me, and I will hearken unto you. (Jeremiah 29:11-12)

Walk in love

Let all that you do be done with love. (I Corinthians 16:14, NKJV)

[1] Though I speak with the tongues of men and of angels, but have not love, I have become sounding brass or a clanging cymbal. [2] And though I have the gift of prophecy, and understand all mysteries and all knowledge, and though I have all faith, so that I could remove mountains, but have not love, I am nothing. And though I bestow all my goods to feed the poor, and though I give my body to be burned, but have not love, it profits me nothing. (I Corinthians 13:1-3, NKJV)

My prayer for you is that you will overflow more and more with love for others, and at the same time keep on growing in spiritual knowledge and insight. (Philippians 1:9, TLB)

Beloved, I wish above all things that thou mayest prosper and be in health, even as thy soul prospereth. (John 2)

CHAPTER X

GOD IS A VERY PRESENT HELP

God is our refuge and strength, a very present help in trouble. (Psalm 46:1, NKJV)

Therefore let all the house of Israel know assuredly, that God hath made that same Jesus, whom ye have crucified, both Lord and Christ. (Acts 2:36)

Mary recognized Jesus as Lord and Christ. Her primary concern was listening to Jesus, learning from Jesus and receiving from Jesus.

> *". . . doesn't it seem unfair to you that my sister just sits here while I do all the work? Tell her to come and help me."*
> *(Luke 10:40, TLB)*

Consequently, when Mary did move, she moved in the wisdom of God. And knew when to serve just as she knew when to receive.

> *{It was that Mary which anointed the Lord with ointment, and wiped his feet with her hair, whose brother Lazarus was sick.}*
> *(John 11:2)*

> *[4] Then saith one of his disciples, Judas Iscariot, Simon's son, which should betray him, [5] Why was not this ointment sold for*

three hundred pence, and given to the poor? (John 12:4-5)

And Jesus said, Let her alone; why trouble ye her? She hath wrought a good work on me. (Mark 14:6)

Verily I say unto you, Wheresover this gospel shall be preached throughout the whole world, this also that she hath done shall be spoken of for a memorial of her. (Mark 14:9)

To walk in the fullness of all that is ours as children of God we must recognize Jesus not only as Savior delivering us from the consequences of our sin, but as Lord and Christ.

[1] The Lord is my shepherd; I shall not want.
[2] He maketh me to lie down in green
pastures: he leadeth me beside the still waters.
[3] He restoreth my soul: he leadeth me in the
paths of righteousness for his name's sake.
[4] Yea, though I walk through the valley of
the shadow of death, I will fear no evil: for
thou art with me; thy rod and thy staff they
comfort me. [5] Thou prepares a table before
me in the presence of mine enemies: thou
anointest my head with oil; my cup runneth
over. [6] Surely goodness and mercy shall
follow me all the days of my life: and I will
dwell in the house of the Lord for ever.
(Psalm 23:1-6)

Christ is not Jesus' surname. It reflects his selection and anointing by God to serve a specific role in our lives. And to accomplish specific things in the earth, in hell and in heaven on our behalf. Lack in the body of Christ is one consequence of having a limited understanding of what the Christ, the "anointed one", was sent to do for us. It is difficult to have faith in something you don't know anything about. Many Christians do refer to Jesus as Lord and Savior. But too often Savior is limited to meaning escape from hell. And Lord is either "*pro forma*" or limited to meaning boss or rule maker. This fails to recognize Jesus as the shepherd, responsible for every aspect of our lives including guidance, protection, and provision. Contrary to what is often misstated as fact, God does not hurt his children, so he can teach them a lesson. Let's not get the roles twisted: pain, destruction, and lack come from Satan; abundance, love, peace, and joy come from Jesus.

> *The thief comes only in order to steal and kill and destroy. I came that they may have and enjoy life, and have it in abundance (to the full, till it overflows). (John 10:10, AMP)*

As the good shepherd his role is to love, guide, protect and provide so that we may have and enjoy an abundant life. Our role is to trust in him, rely on him, follow him, and receive the love, guidance, protection and provision Jesus was anointed to provide.

> *{F}or I seek not yours, but you: for the children ought not to lay up for the parents, but the parents for the children.*
> *(II Corinthians 12:14)*

But often, even Christians who know that as children of God they are entitled – yes, entitled - through the grace of God to receive from God . . .

But Jesus said unto her, Let the children first be filled; for it is not meet to take the children's bread, and to cast it unto the dogs. (Mark 7:27)

. . . put off their expectation to some later time or place. They relegate their receiving to future times or places such as heaven, or the "sweet by and by" instead of the sweet "here and now."

I had fainted, unless I had believed to see the goodness of the Lord in the land of the living. (Psalms 27:13)

When Martha put off God's abundance until the resurrection, Jesus told Martha that He was the resurrection. And just as Jesus was the resurrection then, Jesus is the resurrection now.

[23] Jesus saith unto her, Thy brother shall rise again. [24] Martha saith unto him, I know that he shall rise again in the resurrection at the last day. [25] Jesus said unto her, I am the resurrection, and the life: he that believeth in me, though he were dead, yet shall he live. (John 11:23-25)

[43] And when he thus had spoken, he cried with a loud voice, Lazarus, come forth. [44] And he that was dead came forth, bound hand and foot with graveclothes: and his face was bound about with a napkin. Jesus saith unto them, Loose him, and let him go. (John 11:43-44)

> *Jesus Christ the same yesterday, and to day, and for ever. (Hebrews 13:8)*

The Bible does not say "when you pray, believe you receive someday in the future." Nobody about to have a traffic accident cries "Lord save me from this accident someday." God is always present, and faith is always present tense.

> *[23] For verily I say unto you, That whosoever shall say unto this mountain, Be thou removed, and be thou cast into the sea; and shall not doubt in his heart, but shall believe that those things which he saith shall come to pass; he shall have whatsoever he saith. [24] Therefore I say unto you, What things soever ye desire when ye pray, believe that ye receive them, and ye shall have them. (Mark 11:23-24)*

Recognizing Jesus as Lord and Christ is empowering. It imbues us with trust and expectancy. It emboldens us to draw on and walk in God's power. It assures us that God will be there even if we begin to sink. It enables us to see the love of God. And it uncloaks our spiritual eyes to the revelation that God is love. The love is the power that enables us to do the greater works that Jesus said we would do.

Peter was able to walk on the water because he recognized Jesus as Lord and Christ.

> *[28] And Peter answered him and said, Lord, if it be thou, bid me come unto thee on the water. [29] And he said, Come. And when Peter was come down out of the ship, he*

walked on the water, to go to Jesus.
(Matthew 14:28-29)

The more complacent we are, the more comfortable we are in our discomfort, the more complacent our prayer. The more pedestrian our prayers the more complacently they are likely to be expressed. The Bible speaks about the power of fervent prayer.

> *[16] {T}he effectual fervent prayer of righteous man availeth much. [17] Elias was a man subject to like passions as we are, and he prayed earnestly that it might not rain: and it rained not on the earth by the space of three years and six months. [18] And he prayed again, and the heaven gave rain, and the earth brought forth her fruit. (James 5:16-18)*

When Peter was about to drown, his plea was not complacent.

> *[30] But when he saw the wind boisterous, he was afraid; and beginning to sink, he cried, saying, Lord, save me. [31] And immediately Jesus stretched forth his hand, and caught him, and said unto him, O thou of little faith, wherefore didst thou doubt?*
> *(Matthew 14:30-31)*

The woman with the issue of blood was not complacent. She was sick, broke, and desperate.

> *[43] And a woman having an issue of blood twelve years, which had spent all her living upon physicians, neither could be healed of*

> *any, [44] Came behind him, and touched the border of his garment: and immediately her issue of blood staunched. (Luke 8:43-44)*

Her expectation was not for some uncertain result at some undetermined future time.

> *For she said within herself, If I may touch his garment, I shall be whole. (Matthew 9:22)*

The fervency of her prayer and expectation was so strong that it drew on His power.

> *[30] And Jesus, immediately knowing in himself that virtue had gone out of him, turned him about in the press, and said Who touched my clothes? [31] And his disciples said unto him, Thou seest the multitude thronging thee, and sayest thou, Who touched me? (Mark 5:30-31)*

When we are truly fed up, disgusted, busted, desperate, or in any condition that we recognize as inconsistent with our place as children of God and joint heirs with Christ; when we are determined to have God to bid us to do what we can't do in our own power; or determined to do the greater works Jesus said we would do; then our prayers won't be complacent. They will be fervent and expectant. God is atemporal, he is not subject to time. God created what we call time.[98] The God that dwells in, with and among us, is a very present help.

---

[98] *See Genesis Chapter I*

What agreement {can there be between} a temple of God and idols? For we are the temple of the living God; even as God said, I will dwell in and with and among them and will walk in and with and among them, and I will be their God, and they shall be My people. (II Corinthians 6:16, AMP)

CHAPTER XI

NOW FAITH

Now faith is the substance of things hoped for, the evidence of things not seen. (Hebrews 11:1)

> *Martha saith unto him, I know that he shall rise again in the resurrection at the last day. Jesus said unto her, I am the resurrection . . . (John 11:24-25)*

Jesus is not subject to time . . .

> *I am Alpha and Omega, the beginning and the end, the first and the last. (Revelation 22:13)*

> *Without father, without mother, without descent, having neither beginning of days, nor end of life; but made like unto the Son of God; . . . (Hebrews 7:3)*

. . . nor is the power of faith in the name of Jesus, subject to time.

> *[8] The centurion answered and said, Lord, I am not worthy that thou shouldest come under my roof: but speak the word only, and my servant shall be healed. . .. [10] When Jesus heard it, he marveled, and said to them that followed, Verily I say unto you, I have not found so great faith, no, not in Israel. . ..*

> *[13] And Jesus said unto the centurion, Go thy way; and as thou hast believed, so be it done unto thee. And his servant was healed in the selfsame hour. (Matthew 8:8-13)*

> *For with God nothing shall be impossible. (Luke 1:37)*

When Peter and John spoke in the name of Jesus, the man at the gate called beautiful was immediately healed.

> *[4] And Peter, fastening his eyes upon him with John, said, Look on us. [5] And he gave heed unto them, expecting to receive something of them. [6] Then Peter said, Silver and gold have I none; but such as I have give I thee: In the name of Jesus Christ of Nazareth rise up and walk. [7] And he took him by the right hand, and lifted him up: and immediately his feet and ankle bones received strength. [8] And he leaping up stood, and walked, and entered with them into the temple, walking, and leaping, and praising God. [9] And all the people saw him walking and praising God: (Acts 3:4-9)*

Peter explained to the people present that it was through faith in the name of Jesus, that the man was made whole.

> *[11] And as the lame man which was healed held Peter and John, all the people ran together unto them on the porch that is called Solomon's, greatly wondering. [12] And when Peter saw it, he answered unto the people, Ye men of Israel, why marvel ye at this? Or why*

> *look ye so earnestly on us, as though by our own power of holiness we had made this man to walk? [13] The God of Abraham, and of Isaac, and of Jacob, the God of our fathers, hath glorified his Son Jesus; whom ye delivered up, and denied him in the presence of Pilate, when he was determined to let him go. . . . [16] And his name through faith in his name hath made this man strong, whom ye see and know: yea, the faith which is by him hath given him this perfect soundness in the presence of you all. (Acts 3:11-16)*

God is our source and has already given us all things.

> *According as his divine power hath given unto us all things that pertain unto life and godliness, through the knowledge of him that hath called us to glory and virtue: (2 Peter 1:3)*

> *[30] . . . Christ Jesus, who of God is made unto us wisdom, and righteousness, and sanctification, and redemption; [31] That, according as it is written, He that glorieth, let him glory in the Lord. (I Corinthians 1:30-31)*

Our faith determines our ability to receive what God has already given through the death of Jesus on the cross. The more we know the Word of God, the more we will know the will of God. The more we know the will of God, the greater our faith. And the more we will see the power of God in us (Selah! "in us"), manifested in our lives.

Jesus answered and said unto them, Ye do err, not knowing the scriptures, nor the power of God (Matthew 22:29)

My people are destroyed for lack of knowledge: . . . (Hosea 4:6)

It is a virtuous cycle. The more we grow in knowledge of the Word of God, the more we will hear from God, grow in our knowledge of the will of God and grow in our knowledge of the power of God.

I have still many things to say to you, but you are not able to bear them or to take them upon you or to grasp them now. (John 16:12, AMP)

God has given us the Holy Spirit and the Scriptures so that we can know his will.

All scripture is given by inspiration of God, and is profitable for doctrine, for reproof, for correction, for instruction in righteousness: (2 Timothy 3:16)

But the Comforter {Counselor, Helper, Intercessor, Advocate, Strengthener, Standby} the Holy Spirit, Whom the Father will send in My name {in My place to represent Me and act on My behalf}, He will teach you all things. And He will cause you to recall {will remind you of, bring to your remembrance} everything I have told you. (John 14:26, AMP)

Everything God wants us to "do" or "be", is available to us through the blood of Jesus. And even most of those things that religion (not God, but religion) thinks we should do, be, or earn, God has already made us or provided for us through the blood of Jesus.

The 10 Commandments -

> *[20] The Ten Commandments were given so that all could see the extent of their failure to obey God's laws. But the more we see our sinfulness, the more we see God's abounding grace forgiving us. [21] Before, sin ruled over all men and brought them to death, but now God's kindness rules instead, giving us right standing with God and resulting in eternal life through Jesus Christ our Lord.*
> *(Romans 5:20-21, TLB)*

> *But the fact of the matter is this: when we try to gain God's blessing and salvation by keeping his laws we always end up under his anger for we always fail to keep them. The only way we can keep from breaking laws is not to have any to break!*
> *(Romans 4:15, TLB)*

> *[20] Now do you see it? No one can ever be made right in God's sight by doing what the law commands. For the more we know of God's laws, the clearer it becomes that we aren't obeying them; his laws serve only to make us see that we are sinners. [21-22] But God has shown us a different way to heaven – not by "being good enough" and trying to keep his laws, but by a new way {though not new really, for the Scriptures told about it*

long ago}. Now God says he will accept and acquit us – declare us "Not guilty" – if we trust Jesus Christ to take away our sins. And we all can be saved in this same way, by coming to Christ, no matter who we are or what we have been like. [23] Yes, all have sinned; all fall short of God's glorious idea; [24] yet now God declares us "not guilty" of offending him if we trust in Jesus Christ, who in his kindness freely takes away our sins. [25] For God sent Christ Jesus to take the punishment for our sins and to end all God's anger against us. (Romans 3:20-25, TLB)

The Lord is the Spirit who gives them life, and where he is there is freedom from trying to be saved by keeping the laws of God. (II Corinthians 3:17, TLB)

Abraham's Blessings -

And now that we are Christ's we are the true descendants of Abraham, and all of God's promises to him belong to us. (Galatians 3:29, TLB)

Answered Prayer –

And it shall come to pass, that before they call, I will answer; and while they are yet speaking, I will hear. (Isaiah 65:24)

[14] And this is the confidence that we have in him, that, if we ask any thing according to his will, he heareth us: [15] And if we know that

he hear us, whatsoever we ask, we know that we have the petitions that we desired of him. (1 John 5:14-16)

Children of God –

For ye are all the children of God by faith in Christ Jesus. (Galatians 3:26)

His unchanging plan has always been to adopt us into his own family by sending Jesus Christ to die for us. And he did this because he wanted to! (Ephesians 1:5, TLB)

Condemnation –

[1] So there is now no condemnation awaiting those who belong to Christ Jesus. [2] For the power of the life-giving Spirit – and this power is mine through Christ Jesus – has freed me from the vicious circle of sin and death. [3] We aren't saved from sin's grasp by knowing the commandments of God because we can't and don't keep them, but God put into effect a different plan to save us. He sent his own Son in a human body like ours – except that ours are sinful – and destroyed sin's control over us by giving himself as a sacrifice for our sins. (Romans 8:1-3, TLB)

[33] Who dares accuse us whom God has chosen for his own? Will God? No! He is the one who has forgiven us and given us right standing with himself. [34] Who then will condemn us? Will Christ? No! For he is the

one who died for us and came back to life again for us and is sitting at the place of highest honor next to God, pleading for us there in heaven. (Romans 8:33-34, TLB)

Discerning Spirits –

But now you are meeting people who claim to speak messages from the Spirit of God. How can you know whether they are really inspired by God or whether they are fakes? Here is the test: no one speaking by the power of the Spirit of God can curse Jesus, and no one can say, "Jesus is Lord," and really mean it, unless the Holy Spirit is helping him. (I Corinthians 12:3, TLB)

Eternal Life –

[4] And God has reserved for his children the priceless gift of eternal life; it is kept in heaven for you, pure and undefiled, beyond the reach of change and decay. [5] And God, in his mighty power, will make sure that you get there safely to receive it because you are trusting him. It will be yours in that coming last day for all to see. (I Peter 1:4-5, TLB)

For you have a new life. It was not passed on to you from your parent, for the life they gave you will fade away. This new one will last forever, for it comes from Christ, God's ever-living Message to men. (I Peter 1:23, TLB)

Faith of God –

The faith I speak of is the kind that Jesus Christ our God and Savior gives to us. How precious it is, and how just and good he is to give this same faith to each of us.
(2 Peter 1:1, TLB)

Forgiveness –

[11] For as the heavens are high above the earth, so great is His mercy toward those that fear Him; [12] As far as the east is from the west, so far has He removed our transgressions from us. (Psalm 103:11-12)

*I even I, am he that blotteth out thy transgressions for mine own sake, and will not remember thy sins. (*Isaiah 43:25)

For God was in Christ, restoring the world to himself, no longer counting men's sins against them but blotting them out. This is the wonderful message he has given us to tell others. (II Corinthians 5:19, TLB)

For God says, "Your cry came to me at a favorable time, when the doors of welcome were wide open. I helped you on a day when salvation was being offered." Right now God is ready to welcome you. Today he is ready to save you. (II Corinthians 6:2, TLB)

So overflowing is his kindness toward us that he took away all our sins through the blood of

his Son, by whom we are saved;
(Ephesians 1:7, TLB)

[13] You were dead in sins, and your sinful desires were not yet cut away. Then he gave you a share in the very life of Christ, for he forgave all your sins, [14] and blotted out the charges proved against you, the list of his commandments which you had not obeyed. He took this list of sins and destroyed it by nailing it to Christ's cross. (Colossians 2:13-14, TLB)

Under this new plan we have been forgiven and made clean by Christ's dying for us once and for all. (Hebrews 10:10, TLB)

For by that one offering he made forever perfect in the sight of God all those whom he is making holy. (Hebrews 10:14, TLB)

[16] We have all benefited from the rich blessings he brought to us – blessing upon blessing heaped upon us! [17] For Moses gave us only the Law with its rigid demands and merciless justice, while Jesus Christ brought us loving forgiveness as well.
(John 1:16-17, TLB)

For whatsoever things were written aforetime were written for our learning, that we through patience and comfort of the scriptures might have hope. (Romans 15:4)

[3-4] What a wonderful God we have – he is the Father of our Lord Jesus Christ, the

source of every mercy, and the one who so wonderfully comforts and strengthens us in our hardships and trials. And why does he do this? So that when others are troubled, needing our sympathy and encouragement, we can pass on to them this same help and comfort God has given us. [5] You can be sure that the more we undergo sufferings for Christ, the more he will shower us with his comfort and encouragement. (II Corinthians 1:3-5, TLB)

God's Favor –

{F}or it was through reading the Scripture that I came to realize that I could never find God's favor by trying – and failing – to obey the laws. I came to realize that acceptance with God comes by believing in Christ. (Galatians 2:19, TLB)

Now all praise to God for his wonderful kindness to us and his favor that he has poured out upon us because we belong to his dearly loved Son. (Ephesians 1:6, TLB)

God's Grace –

For while the Law was given through Moses, grace (unearned, undeserved favor and spiritual blessing) and truth came through Jesus Christ. (John 1:17, AMP)

{A}nd he has showered down upon us the richness of his grace – for how well he

understands us and knows what is best for us at all times. (Ephesians 1:8, TLB)

[27] Then what can we boast about doing to earn our salvation? Nothing at all. Why? Because our acquittal is not based on our good deeds; it is based on what Christ has done and our faith in him. [28] So it is that we are saved by faith in Christ and not by the good things we do. (Romans 3:27-28, TLB)

[3] For the Scriptures tell us Abraham believed God, and that is why God canceled his sins and declared him "not guilty."
[4-5] But didn't he earn his right to heaven by all the good things he did? No, for being saved is a gift; if a person could earn it by being good, then it wouldn't be free – but it is! It is given to those who do not work for it. For God declares sinners to be good in his sight if they have faith in Christ to save them from God's wrath. (Romans 4:3-5, TLB)

Thou therefore, my son, be strong in the grace that is in Christ Jesus. (2 Timothy 2:1)

God's Power -

[3] It is true that I am an ordinary, weak human being, but I don't use human plans and methods to win my battles. [4] I use God's mighty weapons, not those made by men, to knock down the devil's strongholds.
(II Corinthians 10:3-6, TLB)

God's Presence –

But now you belong to Christ Jesus, and though you once were far away from God, now you have been brought very near to him because of what Jesus Christ has done for you with his blood. (Ephesians 2:13, TLB)

Now you are no longer strangers to God and foreigners to heaven, but you are members of God's very own family, citizens of God's country, and you belong in God's household with every other Christian.
(Ephesians 2:19, TLB)

Now we can come fearlessly right into God's presence, assured of his glad welcome when we come with Christ and trust in him.
(Ephesians 3:12, TLB)

[9] For in Christ there is all of God in a human body; [10] so you have everything when you have Christ, and you are filled with God throughout your union with Christ. He is the highest Ruler, with authority over every other power. (Colossians 2:9-10, TLB)

{F}or ye are the temple of the living God; as God hath said, I will dwell in them, and walk in them; and I will be their God, and they shall be my people. (II Corinthians 6:16)

[5] For us there is only one Lord, one faith, one baptism, [6] and we all have the same God and Father who is over us all and in us

all, and living through every part of us. (Ephesians 4:5-6, TLB)

God's Provision -

For God, who gives seed to the farmer to plant, and later on good crops to harvest and eat, will give you more and more seed to plant and will make it grow so that you can give away more and more fruit from your harvest. (II Corinthians 9:10, TLB)

Grow in Christ -

[6] I have planted, Apollos watered; but God gave the increase. [7] So then neither is he that planteth any thing, neither he that watereth; but God that giveth the increase. (I Corinthians 3:6-7)

So a person "speaking in tongues" helps himself grow spiritually, but one who prophesies, preaching messages from God, helps the entire church grow in holiness and happiness. (I Corinthians 14:4, TLB)

[5] But also for this very reason, giving all diligence, add to your faith virtue, to virtue knowledge, [6] to knowledge self-control, to self-control perseverance, to perseverance godliness, [7] to godliness brotherly kindness, and to brotherly kindness love. [8] For if these things are yours and abound, you will be neither barren nor unfruitful in the knowledge

of our Lord Jesus Christ.
(2 Peter 1:5-8, NKJV)

Hear from God –

It shall come to pass that before they call, I will answer; and while they are still speaking, I will hear. (Isaiah 65:24, NKJV)

For whatsoever things were written aforetime were written for our learning, that we through patience and comfort of the scriptures might have hope. (Romans 15:4)

In olden times God did not share this plan with his people, but now he has revealed it by the Holy Spirit to his apostles and prophets. (Ephesians 3:5, TLB)

And God has actually given us his Spirit (not the world's spirit) to tell us about the wonderful free gifts of grace and blessing that God has given us. (I Corinthians 2:12, TLB)

Joy -

Hitherto have ye asked nothing in my name: ask, and ye shall receive, that your joy may be full. (John 16:24)

Life after death –

> *And if the Spirit of God, who raised up Jesus from the dead, lives in you, he will make your dying bodies live again after you die, by means of this same Holy Spirit living within you. (Romans 8:11, TLB)*
>
> *Everyone dies because all of us are related to Adam, being members of this sinful race, and wherever there is sin, death results. But all who are related to Christ will rise again. (I Corinthians 15:22, TLB)*
>
> *[44] They are just human bodies at death, but when they come back to life they will be superhuman bodies. For just as there are natural, human bodies, there are also supernatural, spiritual bodies. . . . [46] First, then, we have these human bodies, and later on God gives us spiritual, heavenly bodies. (I Corinthians 15:44-46, TLB)*
>
> *[52] It will all happen in a moment, in the twinkling of an eye, when the last trumpet is blown. For there will be a blast from the sky, and all the Christians who have died will suddenly become alive, with new bodies that will never, never die; and then we who are still alive shall suddenly have new bodies too. [53] For our earthly bodies, the ones we have now that can die, must be transformed into heavenly bodies that cannot perish but will live forever. (I Corinthians 15:52-53, TLB)*

Knowing that he which raised up the Lord Jesus shall raise up us also by Jesus, and shall present us with you. (II Corinthians 4:14)

Love -

Herein is love, not that we loved God, but that he loved us and sent his Son to be the propitiation for our sins. (I John 4:10)

God is love, and anyone who lives in love is living with God and God is living in him. (1 John 4:16, TLB)

Love God –

[2] If anyone thinks he knows all the answers, he is just showing his ignorance. [3] But the person who truly loves God is the one who is open to God's knowledge. (I Corinthians 8:2-3, TLB)

Love of God –

[8] But God showed his great love for us by sending Christ to die for us while we were still sinners. [9] And since by his blood he did all this for us as sinners, how much more will he do for us now that he has declared us not guilty? Now he will save us from all of God's wrath to come. [10] And since, when we were his enemies, we were brought back to God by the death of his son, what blessings he must have for us now that we are his friends and he is living within us! (Romans 5:8-10, TLB)

[38] For I am convinced that nothing can ever separate us from his love. Death can't, and life can't. The angels won't, and all the powers of hell itself cannot keep God's love away. Our fears for today, our worries about tomorrow, [39] or where we are – high above the sky, or in the deepest ocean – nothing will ever be able to separate us from the love of God demonstrated by our Lord Jesus Christ when he died for us. (Romans 8:38-39, TLB)

Mercy –

[4] But God is so rich in mercy; he loved us so much [5] that even though we were spiritually dead and doomed by our sins, he gave us back our lives again when he raised Christ from the dead – only by his underserved favor have we ever been saved – [6] and lifted us up from the grave into glory along with Christ, where we sit with him in the heavenly realms – all because of what Christ Jesus did. (Ephesians 2:4-6, TLB)

Miracles –

I ask you again, does God give you the power of the Holy Spirit and work miracles among you as a result of your trying to obey the Jewish laws? No, of course not. It is when you believe in Christ and fully trust him. (Galatians 3:5, TLB)

[2] But the Jews who spurned God's message stirred up distrust among the Gentiles against Paul and Barnabas, saying all sorts of evil things about them. [3] Nevertheless, they stayed there a long time, preaching boldly, and the Lord proved their message was from him by giving them power to do great miracles. (Acts 14:2-3, TLB)

[11] And God gave Paul the power to do unusual miracles, [12] so that even when his handkerchiefs or parts of his clothing were placed upon sick people, they were healed, and any demons within them came out. (Acts 19:11-12, TLB)

Needs met –

And my God will liberally supply {fill to the full} your every need according to His riches in glory in Christ Jesus. (Philippians 4:19, AMP)

[7] Ask, and it shall be given you; seek, and ye shall find; knock, and it shall be opened unto you: [8] For every one that asketh receiveth; and he that seeketh findeth; and to him that knocketh it shall be opened. (Matthew 7:7-7)

Even when we are too weak to have any faith left, he remains faithful to us and will help us, for he cannot disown us who are part of himself, and he will always carry out his promises to us. (2 Timothy 2:13, TLB)

Obeying God -

> *For God is at work within you, helping you want to obey him, and then helping you do what he wants. (Philippians 2:13, TLB)*

One with Christ -

> *Each of us is a part of the one body of Christ. Some of us are Jews, some are Gentiles, some are slaves, and some are free. But the Holy Spirit has fitted us all together into one body. We have been baptized into Christ's body by the one Spirit, and have all been given that same Holy Spirit. (I Corinthians 12:13, TLB)*

Overcoming temptation –

> *But remember this – the wrong desires that come into your life aren't anything new and different. Many others have faced exactly the same problems before you. And no temptation is irresistible. You can trust God to keep the temptation from becoming so strong that you can't stand up against it, for he has promised this and will do what he says. He will show you how to escape temptation's power so that you can bear up patiently against it. (I Corinthians 10:13, TLB)*

Perfection –

> *[16] All scripture is given by inspiration of God, and is profitable for doctrine, for reproof, for correction, for instruction in righteousness: [17] That the man of God may*

be perfect, thoroughly furnished unto all good works. (II Timothy 3:16-17)

Peace with God -

It was through what his Son did that God cleared a path for everything to come to him – all things in heaven and on earth – for Christ's death on the cross has made peace with God for all by his blood. (Colossians 1:20, TLB)

[22] He has done this through the death on the cross of his own human body, and now as a result Christ has brought you into the very presence of God, and you are standing there before him with nothing left against you – nothing left that he could even chide you for; [23] the only condition is that you fully believe the Truth, standing in it steadfast and firm, strong in the Lord, convinced of the Good News that Jesus died for you, and never shifting from trusting him to save you. (Colossians 1:22-23, TLB)

[1] So now, since we have been made right in God's sight by faith in his promises, we can have real peace with him because of what Jesus Christ our Lord has done for us. [2] For because of our faith, he has brought us into this place of highest privilege where we now stand, and we confidently and joyfully look forward to actually becoming all that God has had in mind for us to be. (Romans 5:1-2, TLB)

Pleasing God -

Moreover, because of what Christ has done, we have become gifts to God that he delights in, for as part of God's sovereign plan we were chosen from the beginning to be his, and all things happen just as he decided long ago. (Ephesians 1:11, TLB)

Dear friends, God the Father chose you long ago and knew you would become his children. And the Holy Spirit has been at work in your hearts, cleansing you with the blood of Jesus Christ and making you to please him. (I Peter 1:2, TLB)

Prayer –

Enter into his gates with thanksgiving, and into his courts with praise: be thankful unto him, and bless his name. (Psalm 100:4)

[9] After this manner therefore pray ye: Our Father which art in heaven, Hallowed be thy name. [10 Thy kingdom come, Thy will be done in earth, as it is in heaven. [11] Give us this day our daily bread. [12] And forgive us our debts, as we forgive our debtors. [13] And lead us not into temptation, but deliver us from evil: For thine is the kingdom, and the power, and the glory, for ever. Amen.
[14] For if ye forgive men their trespasses, your heavenly Father will also forgive you:
[15] But if ye forgive not men their trespasses,

neither will your Father forgive your trespasses. (Matthew 6:9-15)

[7] Ask, and it shall be given you; seek, and ye shall find; knock, and it shall be opened unto you: [8] For every one that asketh receiveth; and he that seeketh findeth; and to him that knocketh it shall be opened. [9] Or what man is there of you, whom if his son ask bread, will he give him a stone? [10] Or if he ask a fish, will he give him a serpent? [11] If ye then, being evil, know how to give good gifts unto your children, how much more shall your Father which is in heaven give good things to them that ask him? (Matthew 7:7-11)

[26] Likewise the Spirit also helpeth our infirmities: for we know not what we should pray for as we ought: but the Spirit itself maketh intercession for us with groanings with cannot be uttered. [27] And he that searcheth the hearts knoweth what is the mind of the Spirit, because he maketh intercession for the saints according to the will of God. [28] And we know that all things work together for good to them that love God, to them who are called according to his purpose. (Romans 8:26-28)

For the eyes of the Lord are over the righteous, and his ears are open unto their prayers: but the face of the Lord is against them that do evil. (I Peter 3:12)

*Let him have all your worries and cares, for he is always thinking about you and watching everything that concerns you.
(I Peter 5:7, TLB)*

Power to bless -

[7] But the manifestation of the Spirit is given to every man to profit withal. [8] For to one is given by the Spirit the word of wisdom; to another the word of knowledge by the same Spirit; [9] To another faith by the same Spirit; to another the gifts of healing by the same Spirit; [10] To another the working of miracles; to another prophecy; to another discerning of spirits; to another divers kinds of tongues; to another the interpretation of tongues; [11] But all these worketh that one and selfsame Spirit, dividing to every man severally as he will. (I Corinthians 12: 7-11)

[7] So let each one give as he purposes in his heart, not grudgingly or of necessity; for God loves a cheerful giver. [8] And God is able to make all grace abound toward you, that you, always having all sufficiency in all things, may have an abundance for every good work. (II Corinthians 9:7-8, NKJV)

Power to heal –

Verily, verily, I say unto you, He that believeth on me, the works that I do shall he do also; and greater works than these shall he do; because I go unto my Father. (John 14:12)

And you no doubt know that Jesus of Nazareth was anointed by God with the Holy Spirit and with power, and he went around doing good and healing all who were possessed by demons, for God was with him.
(Acts 10:38, TLB)

Power to overcome -

Ye are of God, little children, and have overcome them: because greater is he that is in you, than he that is in the world.
(I John 4:4)

[3] It is true that I am an ordinary, weak human being, but I don't use human plans and methods to win my battles. [4] I use God's mighty weapons, not those made by men, to knock down the devil's strongholds.
(II Corinthians 10:3-4, TLB)

Power over sin –

Sin need never again be your master, for now you are no longer tied to the law where sin enslaves you, but you are free under God's favor and mercy. (Romans 6:14, TLB)

He died for our sins just as God our Father planned, and rescued us from this evil world in which we live. (Galatians 1:4, TLB)

But Christ has bought us out from under the doom of that impossible system by taking the curse of our wrongdoing upon himself. For it

is written in the Scripture, "Anyone who is hanged on a tree is cursed" {as Jesus was hung upon a wooden cross}.
(Galatians 3:13, TLB)

[1] So there is now no condemnation awaiting those who belong to Christ Jesus. [2] For the power of the life-giving Spirit – and this power is mine through Christ Jesus – has freed me from the vicious circle of sin and death. [3] We aren't saved from sin's grasp by knowing the commandments of God because we can't and don't keep them, but God put into effect a different plan to save us. He sent his own Son in a human body like ours – except that ours are sinful – and destroyed sin's control over us by giving himself as a sacrifice for our sins. (Romans 8:1-3, TLB)

Protection from evil -

But the Lord is faithful; he will make you strong and guard you from satanic attacks of every kind. (2 Thessalonians 3:3, TLB)

And the Lord shall deliver me from every evil work, and will preserve me unto his heavenly kingdom: to whom be glory for ever and ever. Amen. (2 Timothy 4:18)

[15] "'Who are you, sir?' I asked. "And the Lord replied, 'I am Jesus, the one you are persecuting. [16] Now stand up! For I have appeared to you to appoint you as my servant and my witness. You are to tell the world

about this experience and about the many other occasions when I shall appear to you. [17] And I will protect you from both your own people and the Gentiles. Yes, I am going to send you to the Gentiles to open their eyes to their true condition so that they may repent and live in the light of God instead of in Satan's darkness, so that they may receive forgiveness for their sins and God's inheritance along with all people everywhere whose sins are cleansed away, who are set apart by faith in me.' (Acts 26:15-18, TLB)

Receive God's blessings -

The thief comes only in order to steal and kill and destroy. I came that they may have and enjoy life, and have it in abundance (to the full, till it overflows). (John 10:10, AMP)

[20] I traverse the way of righteousness, in the midst of the path of justice, [21] That I may cause those who love me to inherit wealth, that I may fill their treasuries. (Proverbs 8:20-21, NKJV)

[31] Therefore take no thought, saying, What shall we eat? Or, What shall we drink? or, Wherewithal shall be clothed? [32] {For after all these things do the Gentiles seek:} for your heavenly Father knoweth that ye have need of all these things. [33] But seek ye first the kingdom of God, and his righteousness; and all these things shall be added unto you. (Matthew 6:31-33)

[15] And so we should not be like cringing, fearful slaves, but we should behave like God's very own children, adopted into the bosom of his family and calling to him, "Father, Father." [16] For his Holy Spirit speaks to us deep in our hearts and tells us that we really are God's children. [17] And since we are his children, we will share his treasures – for all God gives to his Son Jesus is now ours too. But if we are to share his glory, we must also share his suffering. (Romans 8:15-17, TLB)

What can we ever say to such wonderful things as these? If God is on our side, who can ever be against us? [32] Since he did not spare even his own Son for us but gave him up for us all, won't he also surely give us everything else? (Romans 8:31, TLB)

And so God's blessings are not given just because someone decides to have them or works hard to get them. They are given because God takes pity on those he wants to. (Romans 9:16, TLB)

May God our Father and the Lord Jesus Christ give you all of his blessings, and great peace of heart and mind.
(I Corinthians 1:3, TLB)

[7] Now you have every grace and blessing; every spiritual gift and power for doing his will are yours during this time of waiting for

the return of our Lord Jesus Christ. [8] And he guarantees right up to the end that you will be counted free from all sin and guilt on that day when he returns. [9] God will surely do this for you, for he always does just what he says, and he is the one who invited you into this wonderful friendship with his Son, even Christ our Lord. (I Corinthians 1:7-9, TLB)

[9] This is what is meant by the Scriptures which say that no mere man has ever seen, heard, or even imagined what wonderful things God has ready for those who love the Lord. [10] But we know about these things because God has sent his Spirit to tell us, and his Spirit searches out and show us all of God's deepest secrets.
(I Corinthians 2:9-10, TLB)

When we ask the Lord's blessing upon our drinking from the cup of wine at the Lord's Table, this means, doesn't it, that all who drink it are sharing together the blessing of Christ's blood? And when we break off pieces of the bread from the loaf to eat there together, this shows that we are sharing together in the benefits of his body.
(I Corinthians 10:16, TLB)

For ye know the grace of our Lord Jesus Christ, that, though he was rich, yet for your sakes he became poor, that ye through his poverty might be rich. (II Corinthians 8:9)

> *[8] And the Scripture, foreseeing that God would justify the heathen through faith, preached before the gospel unto Abraham, saying, In thee shall all nations be blessed. [9] So then they which be of faith are blessed with faithful Abraham. (Galatians 3:8-9)*

> *Now we are no longer slaves but God's own sons. And since we are his sons, everything he has belongs to us, for that is the way God planned. (Galatians 4:7, TLB)*

> *How we praise God, the Father of our Lord Jesus Christ, who has blessed us with every blessing in heaven because we belong to Christ. (Ephesians 1:3, TLB)*

Receive God's peace -

> *[6] Don't worry about anything; instead, pray about everything; tell God your needs, and don't forget to thank him for his answers. [7] If you do this, you will experience God's peace, which is far more wonderful than the human mind can understand. His peace will keep your thoughts and your hearts quiet and at rest as you trust in Christ Jesus. (Philippians 4:6-7, TLB)*

> *[8] Finally, brethren, whatsoever things are true, whatsoever things are honest, whatsoever things are just, whatsoever things are pure, whatsoever things are lovely, whatsoever things are of good report; if there be any virtue, and if there be any praise, think*

on these things. [9] Those things, which ye have both learned, and received, and heard, and seen in me, do: and the God of peace shall be with you. (Philippians 4:8-9)

Receive God's promises -

For as many as are the promises of God, they all find their Yes {answer} in Him {Christ}. For this reason we also utter the Amen {so be it} to God through Him {in His Person and by His agency} to the glory of God.
(II Corinthians 1:20, AMP)

[19] For the Son of God, Jesus Christ, who was preached among you by us, even by me and Silvanus and Timotheus, was not yea and nay, but in him was yea. [20] For all the promises of God in him are yea, and in him Amen, unto the glory of God by us.
(II Corinthians 1:19-20)

Christ came with this new agreement so that all who are invited may come and have forever all the wonders God has promised them. For Christ died to rescue them from the penalty of the sins they had committed while still under that old system.
(Hebrews 9:15, TLB)

Receive the Holy Spirit -

And because we are his sons, God has sent the Spirt of his Son into our hearts, so now we can rightly speak of God as our dear Father. (Galatians 4:6, TLB)

And because of what Christ did, all you others too, who heard the Good News about how to be saved, and trusted Christ, were marked as belonging to Christ by the Holy Spirit, who long ago had been promised to all of us Christians. (Ephesians 1:13, TLB)

Recover from illness –

[16] When the even was come, they brought unto him many that were possessed with devils: and he cast out the spirits with his word, and healed all that were sick: [17] that it might be fulfilled which was spoken by Esaias the prophet, saying, Himself took our infirmities, and bare our sicknesses. (Matthew 8:16-17)

Reign in life -

For if by one man's offence death reigned by one; much more they which receive abundance of grace and of the gift of righteousness shall reign in life by one, Jesus Christ. (Romans 5:17)

Righteousness –

[29] For from the very beginning God decided that those who came to him - and all along he knew who would – should become like his Son, so that his Son would be the First, with many brothers. [30] And having chosen us, he called us to come to him; and when we came, he declared us "not guilty," filled us with Christ's goodness, gave us right standing with himself, and promised us his glory. (Romans 8:29-30, TLB)

Long ago, even before he made the world, God chose us to be his very own through what Christ would do for us; he decided to make us holy in his eyes, without a single fault – we who stand before him covered with his love. (Ephesians 1:4, TLB)

[23] Now this wonderful statement – that he was accepted and approved through his faith – wasn't just for Abraham's benefit. [24] It was for us, too, assuring us that God will accept us in the same way he accepted Abraham – when we believe the promises of God who brought back Jesus our Lord from the dead. [25] He died for our sins and rose again to make us right with God, filling us with God's goodness. (Romans 4:23-25, TLB)

Salvation -

[8] For salvation that comes from trusting Christ – which is what we preach – is already

within easy reach of each of us; in fact, it is as near as our own hearts and mouths. [9] For if you tell others with your own mouth that Jesus Christ is your Lord and believe in your own heart that God has raised him from the dead, you will be saved. [10] For it is by believing in his heart that a man becomes right with God; and with his mouth he tells others of his faith, confirming his salvation.
(Romans 10:8-10, TLB)

[30] For it is from God alone that you have your life through Christ Jesus. He showed us God's plan of salvation; he was the one who made us acceptable to God; he made us pure and holy and gave himself to purchase our salvation. [31] As it says in the Scriptures, "If anyone is going to boast, let him boast only of what the Lord has done."
(I Corinthians 1:30-31, TLB)

The only way out is through faith in Jesus Christ; the way of escape is open to all who believe him. (Galatians 3:22, TLB)

[8] Because of his kindness, you have been saved through trusting Christ. And even trusting is not of yourselves; it too is a gift from God. [9] Salvation is not a reward for the good we have done, so none of us can take any credit for it. (2 Ephesians 8-9, TLB)

[8] Yes, everything else is worthless when compared with the priceless gain of knowing Christ Jesus my Lord. I have put aside all

else, counting it worth less than nothing, in order that I can have Christ, [9] and become one with him, no longer counting on being saved by being good enough or by obeying God's laws, but by trusting Christ to save me; for God's way of making us right with himself depends on faith – counting on Christ alone. (Philippians 3:8-9, TLB)

Sufficiency -

Not that we are sufficient of ourselves to think any thing as of ourselves; but our sufficiency is of God; (II Corinthians 3:5)

Specific individual gifts –

However, Christ has given each of us special abilities – whatever he wants us to have out of his rich storehouse of gifts.
(Ephesians 4:7, TLB)

Trust in God -

For we are the circumcision, which worship God in the spirit, and rejoice in Christ Jesus, and have no confidence in the flesh.
(Philippians 3:3)

Walk in God's power –

[19] I pray that you will begin to understand how incredibly great his power is to help those who believe him. It is that same mighty power [20] that raised Christ from the dead

and seated him in the place of honor at God's right hand in heaven, [21] far, far above any other king or ruler or dictator or leader. Yes, his honor is far more glorious than that of anyone else either in this world or in the world to come. (Ephesians 1:19-21, TLB)

His weak, human body died on the cross, but now he lives by the mighty power of God. We, too, are weak in our bodies, as he was, but now we live and are strong, as he is, and have all of God's power to use in dealing with you. (II Corinthians 13:4, TLB)

Now glory be to God, who by his mighty power at work within us is able to do far more than we would ever dare to ask or even dream of – infinitely beyond our highest prayers, desires, thoughts, or hopes.
(Ephesians 3:20, TLB)

Walk in love –

And hope maketh not ashamed; because the love of God is shed abroad in our hearts by the Holy Ghost which his given unto us.
(Romans 5:5)

Walk in Wisdom -

[15] But the spiritual man has insight into everything, and that bothers and baffles the man of the world, who can't understand him at all. [16] How could he? For certainly he has never been one to know the Lord's

thoughts, or to discuss them with him, or to move the hands of God by prayer. But, . . . we Christians actually do have within us a portion of the very thoughts and mind of Christ. (I Corinthians 2:15-16, TLB)

*[21] So don't be proud of following the wise men of this world. For God has already given you everything you need. [22] He has given you Paul and Apollos and Peter as your helpers. He has given you the whole world to use, and life and even death are our servants. He has given you all of the present and all of the future. All are yours, [23] and you belong to Christ, and Christ is God's.
(I Corinthians 3:21-23, TLB)*

*If any of you lack wisdom, let him ask of God, that giveth to all men liberally, and upbraideth not; and it shall be given him.
(James 1:5)*

Every good thing is available to God's children in the name of Jesus.

For in him dwelleth all the fullness of the Godhead bodily. (Colossians 2:9)

Thank God for his Son – his Gift too wonderful for words. (II Corinthians 9:15, TLB)

CHAPTER XII

BELIEVE THE LOVE

And Simon answering said unto him, Master, we have toiled all the night, and have taken nothing: nevertheless at thy word I will let down the net. And when they had this done, they . . . filled both the ships, so that they began to sink. (Luke 5:5-6)

Now Jesus loved Martha, and her sister, and Lazarus. When he heard therefore that {Lazarus} was sick, he abode two days still in the same place where he was. . . . Then said Jesus unto {his disciples} plainly, Lazarus is dead. And I am glad for your sake that I was not there, to the intent ye may believe; nevertheless let us go unto him. (John 11:5-15)

When we believe the love, we won't accept lack as God's best for our lives.

> *[4] But God, who is rich in mercy, for his great love wherewith he loved us, [5] Even when we were dead in sins, hath quickened us together with Christ,{by grace ye are saved;}. (Ephesians 2:4-5)*

> *Long ago, even before he made the world, God chose us to be his very own through what Christ would do for us; he decided to make us holy in his eyes, without a single fault – we who stand before him covered with his love. (Ephesians 1:4, TLB)*

When we believe the love, we understand that lack is not of God. Lack is not of faith, everything that is not of faith is sin,[99] and wherever sin abounds grace does much more abound.[100] The grace and love of God cannot be separated.

When we believe the love, we won't accept a temporary situation as a permanent condition and thereby fall for Satan's wiles. Evil always attacks at points of real or perceived lack. When Jesus was hungry Satan showed up to tempt Him.

> *[2] And when he had fasted forty days and forty nights, he was afterward an hungered. [3] And when the tempter came to him, he said, If thou be the Son of God, command that these stones be made bread. (Matthew 4:2-3)*

This is the same Jesus that turned water into wine. This is the same Jesus that fed the 5,000 men besides woman and children with five loaves and two fishes and had 12 baskets full remaining.[101] And the same Jesus that fed four thousand men, beside women and children, with seven loaves of bread and a few little fish and had seven baskets full left over.[102]

Jesus didn't succumb to Satan's temptation. Jesus didn't confuse his circumstances with his identity. Jesus didn't confuse a temporary situation with a permanent condition. And Jesus didn't confuse what he had with who he

---

[99] *Romans 14:23*

[100] *Romans 5:20*

[101] *Matthew 14:15-21*

[102] *Matthew 15:32-38*

was. Instead, Jesus believed and leaned on the love of God expressed in the Word of God.

> *But he answered and said, It is written, Man shall not live by bread alone, but by every word that proceedeth out of the mouth of God. (Matthew 4:4)*

> *And he was there in the wilderness forty days, tempted of Satan; and was with the wild beasts; and the angels ministered unto him. (Mark 1:13)*

The more we believe the love of God, the more we will lean on the Word of God. The more we lean on the Word of God, the more we will get the same outcomes that Jesus got. The more we lean on the Word of God, the more we will get the same outcomes that the Word of God says that we will get. The more we lean on the Word of God amidst our weaknesses and wilderness experiences, the more angels will be there to minister unto us just as they were there to minister onto Jesus.

> *Are they not all ministering spirits, sent forth to minister for them who shall be heirs of salvation. (Hebrews 1:14)*

What we believe about the love of God, manifested through Jesus, is the linchpin to our faith.

> *For in Jesus Christ neither circumcision availeth any thing, nor uncircumcision; but faith which worketh by love. (Galatians 5:6)*

And faith is the linchpin to everything we do, will do, won't do, or walk in, as children of God and joint heirs with Christ.

[19] Then came the disciples to Jesus apart, and said, Why could not we cast him out? [20] And Jesus said unto them, Because of your unbelief: for verily I say unto you, If ye have faith as a grain of mustard seed, ye shall say unto this mountain, Remove hence to yonder place; and it shall remove; and nothing shall be impossible unto you. (Matthew 17:19-20)

[24] And they came to him, and awoke him, saying, Master, master, we perish. Then he arose and rebuked the wind and the raging of the water: and they ceased, and there was a calm. [25] And he said unto them Where is your faith? . . . (Luke 8:24-25)

[28] And when he was come into the house, the blind men came to him: and Jesus saith unto them, Believe ye that I am able to do this? They said unto him, Yea, Lord. [29] Then touched he their eyes, saying, According to your faith be it unto you. [30] And their eyes were opened; . . . (Matthew 9:28-30)

Jesus is the Word of God made flesh.

[1] In the beginning was the Word, and the Word was with God, and the Word was God. [2] The same was in the beginning with God. . . [11] He came unto his own, and his own received him not. [12] But as many as received him, to them gave he power to become the sons of God, even to them that believe on his name: . . . [14] And the Word was made flesh, and dwelt among us, {and we beheld his glory, the glory as of the only

> *begotten of the Father,} full of grace and truth. (John 1:2, 11-14)*

> *And he was clothed with a vesture dipped in blood: and his name is called The Word of God. (Revelation 19:13)*

All of the promises in God's word are available to us through the name of Jesus.

> *For as many as are the promises of God, they all find their Yes {answer} in Him {Christ}. . . (II Corinthians 1:20, AMP)*

The more we know the love of God, the power of God, and the promises of the covenant . . .

> *[16] For God so loved the world, that he gave his only begotten Son, that whosoever believeth in him should not perish, but have everlasting life. [17] For God sent not his Son into the world to condemn the world; but that the world through him might be saved. (John 3:16-17)*

> *For with God nothing shall be impossible. (Luke 1:37)*

> *So faith comes by hearing {what is told}, and what is heard comes by the preaching {of the message that came from the lips} of Christ {the Messiah Himself}. (Romans 10:17, AMP)*

. . . the more we will know, believe, and walk in, all that is available to us through the name of Jesus. Believing the love is the foundation of it all.

> *And we have known and believed the love that God hath to us, God is love; and he that dwelleth in love dwelleth in God, and God in him. . . . [19] We love him, because he first loved us. (I John 4:16)*

When we begin to believe the love that is God, we begin to understand the difference between law and grace; the difference between an overseer and a Father; and the difference between sons and servants. Understanding the difference between sons and servants will let us see the love of God for us in the parable of the prodigal son. The son being caused by his circumstances to examine his behavior determined he was not worthy to be called a son and sought to return home to be a servant.

> *[22] But the father said to his servants, Bring forth the best robe, and put it on him; and put a ring on his hand, and shoes on his feet: [23] And bring hither the fatted calf, and kill it; and let us eat, and be merry: [24] For this my son was dead, and is alive again; he was lost, and is found. And they began to be merry. (Luke 15:22-24)*

Similarly, Christians often look at their behavior and try to become servants, instead of believing the love that has made them sons. When we begin to believe the love, we begin to understand that the love is bigger than our past; bigger than our self-proclaimed unrighteousness or unworthiness; bigger than our self-proclaimed goodness; bigger than the bad decisions; bigger than the youthful indiscretions; bigger than the not-so-youthful indiscretions; bigger than the on-purpose choices; bigger than the education or lack of education; and bigger than anything that gives us shame or pride. Whatever we may have done, for good or for ill, the good is not good enough to qualify us for the love, and the bad is not so bad that the love hasn't already covered it.

> *As it is written, There is none righteous, no, not one: (Romans 3:10)*
>
> *For all have sinned, and come short of the glory to God; (Romans 3:23)*
>
> *[38] So let it be clearly known and understood by you, brethren, that through this Man forgiveness and removal of sins is now proclaimed to you; [39] And that through him everyone who believes {who acknowledges Jesus as his Savior and devotes himself to Him} is absolved {cleared and freed} from every charge from which he could not be justified and freed by the Law of Moses and given right standing with God.*
> *(Acts 13:38-39, AMP)*

When we begin to believe the love that is God, we begin to understand why the kingdom of heaven is like the householder that hired men to work in his vineyard and at the end of the day paid the last man he hired the same as he paid the first man he hired.

> *[10] But when the first came, they supposed that they should have received more; and they likewise received every man a penny.*
> *[11] And when they had received it, they murmured against the good man of the house,*
> *[12] Saying, These last have wrought but one hour, and thou has made them equal unto us, which have borne the burden and heat of the day. [13] But he answered one of them, and said, friend, I do thee no wrong; didst not thou*

> *agree with me for a penny? [14] Take that thine is, and go thy way: I will give unto this last, even as unto thee. [15] Is it not lawful for me to do what I will with mine own? Is thine eye evil, because I am good?*
> *(Matthew 20:10-15)*

The love of God is unchanging. God doesn't ration his love. The abundance of God's love for us is not based on when we were born again, or anything that we do, have done, or haven't done. God's love for us is not predicated on any condition or circumstance. The unchanging love of God is exemplified in numerous parables, including the parable of the lost son, the parable of the lost sheep, and the parable of the woman with the lost coin.

> *[25] Now his elder son was in the field: and as he came and drew nigh to the house, he heard musick and dancing. [26] And he called one of the servants, and asked what these things meant. [27] And he said unto him, Thy brother is come; and thy father hath killed the fatted calf, because he hath received him safe and sound. [28] And he was angry, and would not go in: therefore came his father out, and entreated him. [29] And he answering said to his father, Lo, these many years do I serve thee, neither transgressed I at any time thy commandment: and yet thou never gavest me a kid, that I might make merry with my friends: [30] But as soon as this thy son was come, which hath devoured thy living with harlots, thou has killed for him the fatted calf. [31] And he said unto him, Son, thou art ever with me, and all that I have is thine. [32] It was meet that we should make merry, and be glad: for this thy brother was dead, and is*

> *alive again; and was lost, and is found. (Luke 15:25-32)*
>
> *[4] What man of you, having an hundred sheep, if he lose one of them, doth not leave the ninety and nine in the wilderness, and go after that which is lost, until he find it. [5] And when he hath found it, he layeth it on his shoulders, rejoicing. [6] And when he cometh home, he calleth together his friends and neighbours, saying unto them, Rejoice with me; for I have found my sheep which was lost. [7] I say unto you likewise joy shall be in heaven over one sinner that repenteth, more than over ninety and nine just persons, which need no repentance. (Luke 15:4-7)*
>
> *[8] Either what woman having ten pieces of silver, if she lose one piece, doth not light a candle, and sweep the house, and seek diligently till she find it? [9] And when she hath found it, she calleth her friends and her neighbours together, saying, Rejoice with me; for I have found the piece which I had lost. [10] Likewise, I say unto you, there is joy in the presence of the angels of God over one sinner that repenteth. (Like 15:8-10)*

When we begin to believe the love, we begin to see that Jesus not only preached the love of God, he lived it, and he demonstrated it for us. Every miracle, every healing, every drop of wine created, and every drop of blood spilt, was a demonstration and manifestation of the love. Health, peace, spiritual, physical and financial abundance are all manifestations of the love of God, and the love that is God.

Everything we need is in the love.

> *[31] Therefore take no thought, saying, What shall we eat? Or What shall we drink? or, Wherewithal shall we be clothed? [32] (For after all these things do the gentiles seek:) for your heavenly Father knoweth that ye have need of all these things. [33] But seek ye first the kingdom of God, and his righteousness; and all these things shall be added unto you. (Matthew 6:31-33)*

Everything we desire is in the love.

> *Therefore I say unto you, What things soever ye desire, when ye pray, believe that ye receive them, and ye shall have them. (Mark 11:24)*

The love of God is eternal, just as God is eternal.

> *[38] For I am persuaded, that neither death, nor life, nor angels, nor principalities, nor powers, nor things present, nor things to come, [39] Nor heights, nor depth, nor any other creature, shall be able to separate us from the love of God, which is in Christ Jesus our Lord. (Romans 8:38-39)*

> *Now unto the King eternal, immortal, invisible, the only wise God, be honour and glory for ever and ever. Amen. (I Timothy 1:17)*

Not because we loved God, but because he loved us.

Herein is love, not that we loved God, but that he loved us, and sent his Son to be the propitiation for our sins. (I John 4:10)

[16] For God so loved the world, that he gave his only begotten Son, that whosoever believeth in him should not perish, but have everlasting life. [17] For God sent not his Son into the world to condemn the world; but that the world through him might be saved. (John 3:16-17)

When we begin to believe the love, we begin to understand that our prayers and expectations of receiving do not have to be limited to desperate times of sickness, disease, lack, danger, or any other negative conditions or circumstances. God wants us to live and enjoy life.

The thief comes only in order to steal and kill and destroy. I came that they may have and enjoy life, and have it in abundance (to the full, till it overflows). (John 10:10, AMP)

In fact, the Bible says God gives us all things to enjoy.

Charge them that are rich in this world, that they be not highminded, nor trust in uncertain riches, but in the living God, who giveth us richly all things to enjoy; (I Timothy 6:17)

God doesn't have to specifically say you can have a nice car any more than he has to specifically say you can have air. There is no difference in the love that provides one and the love that provides the other.

If ye then, being evil, know how to give good gifts unto your children, how much more shall your Father which is in heaven give good things to them that ask him? (Matthew 7:11)

As the father in the parable of the prodigal son made his sons heirs of all he had, God through Christ has made us heirs of all he has. And God has the entire world.

Behold, what manner of love the Father hath bestowed upon us, that we should be called the sons of God: . . . (I John 3:1)

[5] Not by works of righteousness which we have done, but according to his mercy he saved us, by the washing of regeneration, and renewing of the Holy Ghost; [6] Which he shed on us abundantly through Jesus Christ our Saviour; [7] That being justified by his grace, we should be made heirs according to the hope of eternal life. (Titus 3:5-7)

And if ye be Christ's, then are ye Abraham's seed, and heirs according to the promise. (Galatians 3:29)

For the promise, that he should be heir of the world, was not to Abraham, or to his seed, through the law, but through the righteousness of faith. (Romans 4:13)

[29] And Jesus answered and said, Verily I say unto you, There is no man that hath left house, or brethren, or sisters, or father, or mother, or wife, or children, or lands, for my

sake and the gospel's, [30] But he shall receive an hundredfold now in this time, houses, and brethren, and sisters, and mothers, and children, and lands, with persecutions; and in the world to come eternal life. (Mark 10:29-30)

The same love provides us with the inanimate material things and animated spiritual power.

I can do all things through Christ which strengtheneth me. (Philippians 4:13)

[17] And these signs shall follow them that believe; In my name shall they cast out devils; they shall speak with new tongues; [18] They shall take up serpents; and if they drink any deadly thing, it shall not hurt them; they shall lay hands on the sick, and they shall recover. (Mark 16:17-18)

[19] Behold, I give unto you power to tread on serpents and scorpions, and over all the power of the enemy: and nothing shall by any means hurt you. [20] Notwithstanding in this rejoice not, that the spirits are subject unto you; but rather rejoice, because your names are written in heaven. (Luke 10:19-20)

Blessed be the God and Father of our Lord Jesus Christ, who hath blessed us with all spiritual blessings in heavenly places in Christ: (Ephesians 1:3)

The love is set forth in the word. Jesus is the word made flesh. We have access to the love set forth in the word through the name of Jesus. And when we receive Jesus, we receive the Father who is love.

> *He that receiveth you receiveth me, and he that receiveth me receiveth him that sent me. (Matthew 10:40)*

When we receive the Son of God, in the name of the Son of God, we receive the reward of the Son of God. We have no righteousness of our own, so we can receive no reward of our own. The only reward we can possibly receive is every reward that Jesus Christ the Son of God is entitled to receive. Hallelujah!!

> *He that receiveth a prophet in the name of a prophet shall receive a prophet's reward; and he that receiveth a righteous man in the name of a righteous man shall receive a righteous man's reward. (Matthew 10:41)*

> *[14] For as many as are led by the Spirit of God, they are the sons of God. . . [16] The Spirit itself beareth witness with our spirit, that we are the children of God: [17] And if children, then heirs; heirs of God, and joint-heirs with Christ; . . . (Romans 8:14-17)*

> *{W}orthy is the Lamb that was slain to receive power, and riches, and wisdom, and strength, and honour, and glory, and blessing. (Revelation 5:12)*

And we are his joint heirs. Now pause and think about that!!!

[17] In this {union and communion with Him} love is brought to completion and attains perfection with us, that we may have confidence for the day of judgment {with assurance and boldness to face Him}, because as He is, so are we in this world. (I John 4:17, AMP)

CHAPTER XIII

WHATSOEVER THOU SHALL ASK

But I know, that even now, whatsoever thou will ask of God, God will give it thee. (John 11:22)

A man who was financially destitute and in ill health, turned to a lunch companion and said, "God never promised you a BMW." At that time, the man that made the statement had been pastoring and speaking in churches for over 30 years. Lamenting his own physical, financial, and familial poverty while speaking with a friend away from the crowd at the table, this same man said he didn't know why God had done this to him.

Wow!

There is a direct connection between our beliefs and our conditions. If we are to walk in the fullness of our inheritance as children of God, it is vitally important that we understand that the quality of our Christian lives depends on what we say/ask and on what we believe/expect.

> *Death and life are in the power of the tongue, . . . (Proverbs 18:21, NKJV)*
>
> *A man shall eat well by the fruit of his mouth, . . . (Proverbs 13:2, NKJV)*
>
> *Now the just shall live by faith: . . . (Hebrews 10:38)*

What we say/ask evidences what we believe/expect and directly impacts what we receive/walk in. It dictates how much of our inheritance – which Jesus died for us to receive – will be manifested in our lives.

> *A good man out of the good treasure of the heart bringeth forth good things; and an evil man out of the evil treasure bringeth forth evil things. (Matthew 12:35)*

> *We having the same spirit of faith, according as it is written, 'I believed,*
> *and therefore have I spoken; we also believe, and therefore speak; (II Corinthians 4:13)*

> *[1] Now faith is the substance of things hoped for, the evidence of things not seen. [2] For by it the elders obtained a good report.*
> *(Hebrews 11:1-2)*

Of the Israelites that God specifically sent Moses to lead to the promised land, those that didn't have a good report NEVER entered the promised land.

> *[30] Then Caleb quieted the people before Moses, and said, "Let us go up at once and take possession, for we are well able to overcome it." [31] But the men who had gone up with him said, "We are not able to go up against the people, for they are stronger than we." [32] And they gave the children of Israel a bad report of the land which they had spied out, . . . (Numbers 13:30-32, NKJV)*

> *[36] Now the men whom Moses sent to spy out the land, who returned and made all the congregation complain against him by bringing a bad report of the land, [37] those very men who brought the evil report about the land died by the plague before the Lord. [38] But Joshua the son of Nun and Caleb the son of Jephunneh remained alive, of the men who went to spy out the land. (Numbers 14:36-38, NKJV)*

What we say/ask bares evidence what we believe/expect and either rejects God or releases the positive power of God on our behalf into every area and circumstance of our spiritual and physical lives.

What we believe and say is how we are saved - *aka* born again - as possessors of eternal life.

> *[8] But what saith it? The word is nigh thee, even in thy mouth, and in thy heart: that is, the word of faith, which we preach; [9] That if thou shalt confess with thy mouth the Lord Jesus, and shalt believe in thine heart that God hath raised him from the dead, thou shalt be saved. [10] For with the heart man believeth unto righteousness; and with the mouth confession is made unto salvation. (Romans 10:8-10)*

> *For whoever shall call upon the Lord shall be saved. (Romans 10:13)*

Once we are born again, the Bible tells us to come boldly before God.

Let us therefore come boldly unto the throne of grace, that we may obtain mercy, and find grace to help in time of need. (Hebrews 4:16)

And when we boldly come to God, what we believe matters.

But without faith it is impossible to please him: for he that cometh to God must believe that he is, and that he is a rewarder of them that diligently seek him. (Hebrews 11:6)

The same faith that made us children of God, gives us peace with God, and allows us to walk in the grace and favor of God.

Therefore being justified by faith, we have peace with God through our Lord Jesus Christ: (Romans 5:1)

Through Him also we have {our} access {entrance, introduction} by faith into this grace {state of God's favor} in which we {firmly and safely} stand. And let us rejoice and exult in our hope of experiencing and enjoying the glory to God.
(Romans 5:2, AMP)

It is through our faith/what we believe that we are filled with the Holy Spirit and with power.

[38] He that believeth on me, as the scripture hath said, out of his belly shall flow rivers of living water. [39] {But this spake he of the

Spirit, which they that believe on him should receive: for the Holy Ghost was not yet given; because that Jesus was not yet glorified.} (John 7:38-39)

And we also {especially} thank God continually for this, that when you received the message of God {which you heard} from us, you welcomed it not as the word of {mere} men, but as it truly is, The Word of God, which is effectually at work in you who believe {exercising its super-human power in those who adhere to and trust in and rely on it}. (1Thessalonians 2:13, AMP)

And the Holy Spirit bears witness that we are adopted children of God, and joint heirs with Christ.

[4] But when the fullness of the time was come, God sent forth his Son, made of a woman, made under the law, [5] To redeem them that were under the law, that we might receive the adoption of sons. [6] And because ye are sons God hath sent forth the Spirit of his Son into your hearts, crying Abba, Father. (Galatians 4:4-6)

[14] For all who are led by the Spirit of God are sons of God. [15] For {the Spirit which} you have now received {is} not a spirit of slavery to put you once more in bondage to fear, but you have received the Spirit of adoption {the Spirit producing sonship} in {the bliss of} which we cry Abba {Father}! Father! (Romans 8:14-15, AMP)

And if children, then heirs; heirs of God, and joint-heirs with Christ; . . . (Romans 8:17)

The Holy Spirit also gives us revelation of our inheritance in Christ.

[9] But as it is written, Eye hath not seen, nor ear heard, neither have entered into the heart of man, the things which God hath prepared for them that love him. [10] But God hath revealed them unto us by his Spirit: . . . (I Corinthians 2:9-10)

Now we have received, not the spirit of the world, but the spirit which is of God; that we might know the things that are freely given to us of God. (I Corinthians 2:12)

It is by faith/what we believe that we are the children of Abraham entitled to the promises of Abraham.

[6] Even as Abraham believed God, and it was accounted to him for righteousness.
[7] Know ye therefore that they which are of faith, the same are the children of Abraham. (Galatians 3:6-7)

For the promise, that he should be heir of the world, was not to Abraham, or to his seed, through the law, but through the righteousness of faith. (Romans 4:13)

So then they which be of faith are blessed with faithful Abraham. (Galatians 3:9)

What we believe determines whether we see, and how much we see, the glory and miracles of God manifested in our lives.

> *Jesus saith unto her, Said I not unto thee, that, if thou wouldest believe, thou shouldest see the glory of God? (John 11:40)*

What we say and believe is how we receive what we ask for in prayer. And when we don't know what to pray the Holy Spirit intercedes/speaks on our behalf.

> *And all things, whatsoever ye shall ask in prayer, believing, ye shall receive. (Matthew 21:22)*

> *Likewise the Spirit also helpeth our infirmities: for we know not what we should pray for as we ought: but the Spirit itself maketh intercession for us with groanings which cannot be uttered. (Romans 8:26)*

We have the ability, by what we say, to manifest both blessings and curses in our lives.

> *Out of the same mouth proceedeth blessing and cursing. . . (James 3:10)*

> *Not that which goeth into the mouth defileth a man; but that which cometh out of the mouth, this defileth a man. (Matthew 15:11)*

> *[20] And in the morning, as they passed by, they saw the fig tree dried up from the roots.*

> *[21] And Peter calling to remembrance saith unto him, Master, behold, the fig tree which thou cursedst is withered away.*
> *(Mark 11:20-21)*

> *[21] Jesus answered and said unto them, Verily I say unto you, If ye have faith, and doubt not, ye shall not only do this which is done to the fig tree, but also if ye shall say unto this mountain, Be thou removed, and be thou cast into the sea; it shall be done.*
> *[22] And all things, whatsoever ye shall ask in prayer, believing, ye shall receive.*
> *(Matthew 21:21-22)*

What we say and believe is how we make manifest material things - of whatever sort - in our lives.

> *Through faith we understand that the worlds were framed by the Word of God, so that things which are seen were not made of things which do appear. (Hebrews 11:3)*

> *For the eyes of the Lord are over the righteous, and his ears are open unto their prayers . . . (I Peter 3:12)*

> *[14] And this is the confidence that we have in him, that, if we ask any thing according to his will, he heareth us: [15] And if we know that he hear us, whatsoever we ask, we know that we have the petitions that we desired of him.*
> *(I John 5:14-15)*

What we say and believe is how we move the mountains of whatever sort – spiritual, physical, or financial - in our lives.

> *[17] Elias was a man subject to like passions as we are, and he prayed earnestly that it might not rain; and it rained not on the earth by the space of three years and six months. [18] And he prayed again, and the heaven gave rain, and the earth brought forth her fruit. (James 5:17-18)*

> *For verily I say unto you, That whosoever shall say unto this mountain, Be thou removed, and be thou cast into the sea; and shall not doubt in his heart, but shall believe that those things which he saith shall come to pass; he shall have whatsoever he saith. (Mark 11:23)*

What we say/ask and believe is how the sick are healed.

> *And the prayer of faith shall save the sick, and the Lord shall raise him up; and if he have committed sins, they shall be forgiven him. (James 5:15)*

> *[5-6] When Jesus arrived in Capernaum, a Roman army captain came and pled with him to come to his home and heal his servant boy who was in bed paralyzed and racked with pain. [7] "Yes," Jesus said, "I will come and heal him." [8-9] Then the officer said, "Sir, I am not worthy to have you in my home; and it*

> *isn't necessary for you to come. If you will only stand here and say, 'Be healed,' my servant will get well! I know, because I am under the authority of my superior officers and I have authority over my soldiers, and I say to one, 'Go,' and he goes, and to another, 'Come,' and he comes, and to my slave boy 'Do this or that,' and he does it. And I know you have authority to tell his sickness to go – and it will go!" [10] Jesus stood there amazed! Turning to the crowd he said, "I haven't seen faith like this in all the land of Israel! . . . [13] Then Jesus said to the Roman officer, "Go on home. What you have believed has happened!" And the boy was healed that same hour!*
> *(Matthew 8:5-13, TLB)*

What we say and believe is how we receive wisdom from God.

> *If any of you lack wisdom, let him ask of God, that giveth to all men liberally, and upbraideth not; and it shall be given him. [6] But let him ask in faith, nothing wavering. For he that wavereth is like a wave of the sea driven with the wind and tossed. (James 1:5)*

And the wisdom of God enables us to do mighty acts. Even greater acts than Jesus did.

> *And when he was come into his own country, he taught them in their synagogue, insomuch that they were astonished, and said, Whence*

> *hath this man this wisdom, and these mighty works? (Matthew 13:54)*
>
> *Verily, verily, I say unto you, He that believeth on me, the works that I do shall he do also; and greater works than these shall he do; because I go unto my Father. (John 14:12)*

There is nothing we can ask or imagine that is too hard for God.

> *Now glory be to God, who by his mighty power at work within us is able to do far more than we would ever dare to ask or even dream of – infinitely beyond our highest prayers, desires, thoughts or hopes.*
> *(Ephesians 3:20, TLB)*

In fact, the Bible directs us to ask, and affirms the truth that God will answer our prayers and provide us good things - plural.

> *[7] Ask, and it shall be given you; seek, and ye shall find; knock, and it shall be opened unto you: [8] For every one that asketh receiveth; and he that seeketh findeth; and to him that knocketh it shall be opened. (Matthew 7:7-8)*
>
> *If ye then, being evil, know how to give good gifts unto your children, how much more shall your Father which is in heaven give good things to them that ask him? (Matthew 7:11)*

We make the choice, by what we say and believe, to walk in the power of God.

[28] Then said they unto him, What shall we do, that we might work the works of God? [29] Jesus answered and said unto them, This is the work of God, that ye believe on him whom he hath sent. (John 6:28-29)

For whatsoever is born of God overcometh the world: and this is the victory that overcometh the world, even our faith. (1 John 5:4)

What we do reflects what we believe.

Was not our forefather Abraham {shown to be} justified (made acceptable to God) by {his} works when he brought to the altar as an offering his {own} son Isaac. (James 2:21, AMP)

And {so} the Scripture was fulfilled that says, Abraham believed in {adhered to, trusted in, and relied on} God, and this was accounted to him as righteousness {as conformity to God's will in thought and deed}, and he was called God's friend. (James 2:23, AMP)

What we believe reflects who we are.

Whosoever believeth that Jesus is the Christ is born of God . . . (1 John 5:1)

What we say makes what we believe manifest in our lives. Author Francis P. Martin, in the book *Hung by the Tongue,* said:

> *This is how we obtain the great and precious promises: prosperity, health, deliverance, rest, peace of mind, victory and authority over Satan. Jesus already has obtained the victory. We only have to confess it for ourselves, agree with Him, that I am an overcomer, more than a conqueror, a wonder unto many, can do all things, have all things, etc. Whatever the Word says, I say in Jesus' Name – and then He says it for me before the Father – Hallelujah! For example, just as your salvation was wrought on the cross 2,000 years ago, you didn't receive it until you confessed it. So, also, our complete inheritance was paid for and obtained 2,000 years ago, but we only receive it as we confess it.*[103]

---

[103] Francis P. Martin, *Hung by the Tongue, p. 49.*

CHAPTER XIV

I WILL BLESS THE LORD

And she had a sister called Mary, which also sat at Jesus' feet, and heard his word. (Luke 10:39)

Come, see a man, which told me all things that ever I did: is not this the Christ? (John 4:29)

When we sit at the feet of Jesus, receiving from Jesus, like Mary; and when we draw from Jesus, like the Samaritan woman at the well; Jesus is doing the will of the Father. And when Jesus is doing the will of his Father, Jesus is being fed.

> *[34] Jesus saith unto them, My meat is to do the will of him that sent me, and to finish his work. (John 4:34)*

When Martha had gone off to prepare food, Jesus was being fed by Mary sitting at his feet hearing and believing the word of the Lord. When the disciples had gone off to buy food, Jesus was being fed by the woman at the well hearing and believing the word of the Lord. On the Mount of Transfiguration God didn't say this is my beloved son, feed him. He said this is my beloved Son, hear him.

> *[4] And there appeared unto them Elias with Moses: and they were talking with Jesus. [5] And Peter answered and said to Jesus, Master, it is good for us to be here: and let us make three tabernacles; one for thee, and one for Moses, and one for Elias. [6] For he wist not what to say; for they were sore afraid.*

[7] And there was a cloud that overshadowed them: and a voice came out of the cloud, saying, This is my beloved Son: hear him. (Mark 9:4-7)

There is a well-intended but poverty inducing mindset that hinders Christians from receiving the abundance of God that is ours through faith in the name of Jesus; that is ours as joint heirs with Christ; and that has been set aside for us. Because of this mindset we try to create through our works what we should be receiving through our faith in the name of Jesus, who was not sent to be ministered unto but to minister unto.

Even as the Son of man came not to be ministered unto, but to minister, and to give his life a ransom for many. (Matthew 20:28)

For whether is greater, he that sitteth at meat, or he that serveth? Is not he that sitteth at meat? But I am among you as he that serveth. (Luke 22:27)

For God sent Christ Jesus to take the punishment for our sins and to end all God's anger against us. (Romans 3:25, TLB)

Who was delivered for our offences, and was raised again for our justification. (Romans 4:25)

For God so loved the world, that he gave his only begotten Son, that whosoever believeth in him should not perish, but have everlasting life. (John 3:16)

The more we stop relying on our toil and start relying on the Word of God, the more we will walk in the abundance of God.

> *[5] Master we have toiled all night, and have taken nothing: nevertheless at thy word I will let down the net. [6] And when they had this done, they inclosed a great multitude of fishes: and their net brake. (Luke 5:5-6)*

> *{I}t is written, That man shall not live by bread along, but by every Word of God. (Luke 4:4)*

> *Now ye are clean through the word which I have spoken unto you. (John 15:3)*

When we rely on the Word of God, righteousness and blessedness is ours through faith in the name of Jesus.

> *[5] But to him that worketh not, but believeth on him that justifieth the ungodly, his faith is counted for righteousness. [6] Even as David also describeth the blessedness of man, unto whom God imputeth righteousness without works . . . [8] Blessed is the man to whom the Lord will not impute sin. (Romans 4:5-8)*

And when we hear and are blessed through the Word of God, Jesus is fed because he is doing the will of his Father.

> *[18] The Spirit of the Lord is upon me, because he hath anointed me to preach the gospel to the poor; he hath sent me to heal the brokenhearted, to preach deliverance to the*

> *captives, and recovering of sight to the blind, to set at liberty them that are bruised. [19] To preach the acceptable year of the Lord. (Luke 4:18-19)*

And she had a sister called Mary, which also sat at Jesus' feet, and heard his word. But Martha was cumbered about much serving, and came to him, and said, Lord, dost thou not care that my sister hath left me to serve alone? Bid her therefore that she help me. And Jesus answered and said unto her, Martha, Martha, thou art careful and troubled about many things: But one thing is needful: and Mary hath chosen that good part, which shall not be taken away from her. (Luke 10:39-42)

ABOUT THE AUTHOR

JAMES W. FERGUSON, J.D., M.A.

James Ferguson has served as an advisor to executives and achievers in the sports, music, and telecommunications industries, to pastors and to public servants for more than twenty years. He is a prolific writer and ghostwriter. One of his daily goals is to develop leaders of leaders and leaders of organizations. In collaborating with church leaders, his focus is on growing and maturing the body of Christ. James often laughs when others look at his background and see a logical planned progression from one success to the next.

"I've made enough mistakes along the way, for me and for a lot of others. And there have been as many deep valleys as there have been peaks. I don't wish the valleys on anybody. Although, for me, the valleys played an important role in my maturation process, in normalizing the fundamentals of success, in understanding the importance of pouring into others, and my reliance on God. More importantly, the grace of God has used each step, and placed special people along my path. Each of these have helped me to grow, to develop a commitment to continuous learning, and a commitment to developing others."

When asked about whether there was any one thing that he believe makes the difference in our growth as Christians, James said: "Understanding that it is not about our perfection. It is about recognition and reliance on His perfection."

James Ferguson has a Juris Doctor from Howard University School of Law, and a M.A. in Executive Leadership from Liberty University, School of Business. James describes himself as a child of God, a developer of people, and a Native New Yorker. He currently lives in the Washington, D.C. area. Please contact James' via his website at www.JamesWFerguson.com or search for him on Facebook @AuthorJamesWFerguson.

Book Mr. Ferguson to speak at your event at his website!

www.JamesWFerguson.com

James W. Ferguson, JD

@AuthorJamesWFerguson · Author

+ Add a Button

Connect with Mr. Ferguson on FaceBook!!

www.FaceBook.com/AuthorJamesWFerguson

www.ingramcontent.com/pod-product-compliance
Lightning Source LLC
LaVergne TN
LVHW020709110826
845149LV00012B/2180

* 9 7 8 0 9 9 8 1 6 9 0 2 6 *